RAGS TO RICHES
The Story of the Companions of Emmaus

Henri Le Boursicaud

VERITAS

Published 1991 by
Veritas Publications
7-8 Lower Abbey Street
Dublin 1

Original French language edition of
Compagnons d'Emmaüs
published and copyright 1979 by
Les Éditions du Cerf
29 Blvd Latour-Maubourg
Paris
France

ISBN 1 85390 053 2

Translation by Josephine O'Donovan
Cover design by Banahan McManus, Dublin
Typesetting by Printset & Design Ltd, Dublin
Printed in the Republic of Ireland by
Leinster Leader Ltd, Naas

To all my family at Elven
To all Companions of Emmaus
To all those who have suffered and who are suffering still
To all my friends
To all who have helped me
And especially to Francois Bourdeau,
a friend,
who has helped me greatly in the writing of this book.

Faced with all human suffering, according to your capabilities seek not only to alleviate it without delay but also to root out and destroy its causes.

Seek not only to destroy its causes but also to alleviate it without delay.

Nobody is truly good or just or true unless he dedicates himself, to the best of his capabilities, with his whole heart and his whole being to both of these tasks. They cannot be separated without destroying each other.

Extract from the
Rule of Life for the Companions of Emmaus

Contents

Preface *by* Roger Cardinal Etchegaray   7

Foreword *by* Raphael Gallagher CSsR   9

Introduction   11

Prologue   15

1. We are not beggars   20

2. They have suffered   33

3. The three beginnings of Emmaus   40

4. Friendship that is stronger than death   53

5. A house of hope   75

6. People of love and understanding   89

7. Emmaus: alibi or provocation?   101

8. The future of Emmaus   112

Epilogue: Seventeen years later   127

Preface

The Catholic philosopher Jean Guitton was once asked: 'If you were to lose your memory, which page from the Gospels would you like to be able to save from oblivion?' He replied without hesitation, 'The story of the Companions of Emmaus.' Each one of us is called to follow the Emmaus road, to live the message of Easter as we walk, as we talk to one another, as we open our eyes to the mystery of the breaking of the living bread.

This book tells one of the stories of Emmaus, lived not by two people as on the evening of the first Easter, but lived by tens, hundreds of people. The more we share poverty and seek solutions together, the greater will be our discovery, our joy, and the more our hearts will burn within us.

I would like to thank Fr Henri Le Boursicaud, the courageous Redemptorist missionary, for telling us of the experiences and exploits of the founder of the Emmaus communities, the famous 'Abbé Pierre'. However, in addition to his own experiences, we see those of so many Companions whom he has helped to put on their feet again, and to walk the Emmaus road.

It is my hope that these pages may awaken many hopeful adventurers. Hope does not express itself through official decrees and orders, but through walking with the movement. The world has more need than ever of these prophets of a 'God who is coming' and for whom we would not be waiting if we were not sure that he has already come. And God chooses these prophets from among the poorest and the most destitute.

I am reminded of the words of Charles Péguy:

> We wonder, we say: 'But how is it
> that this ancient fountain flows eternally,
> eternally young, fresh, alive....
>
> It must have a secret of its own.'
>
> 'Good people,' says God, 'it's very simple.
> If it was from pure water that it tried to bring
> forth these pure waters,
> it would never find enough in all of my creation.
> But it is precisely with impure water that it makes pure
> springs.
> And that is why it never runs short.
> And that also is why it is Hope.
> And it is the most beautiful secret in the garden of the
> world.

Yes, and it is also the most beautiful secret of the Companions of Emmaus.

Rome, 4 October 1988
Feast of Saint Francis of Assisi

Roger Cardinal Etchegaray

Foreword

Builders will often tell you that it is better to spend your money on a new house rather than trying to renovate old ones: throwing good money after bad, they say.

I have a sense that many of the religious structures of the house that is Irish Catholicism are creaking. A lot of effort and money is being put into renewing those old structures.

The new may be somewhere else.

This story of the Companions of Emmaus gives a glimpse of how that new can happen. Poor people help poor people, not out of pity or mere charity, but because these poor people have confidence in and respect for each other. Each Companion's story tells something about bruised hearts, battered bodies and bewildered souls that, together, create a new hope and respect for each other.

The poor will inherit the earth. The Companions of Emmaus are neither a charitable organisation nor a political party: they have a spark of that original gospel simplicity, or naivete if you wish to dismiss them. It is possible to challenge the sinful waste, stupid egoism and thoughtless consumerism of our times. They do not offer a sanctuary from the realities of life: being with and among the poor, they help lessen the poverty of the poorest and at the same time try to tackle the unjust structures that cause that poverty in the first place.

We, Irish Catholics, are often too caught up in the struggle for power, control and comfort. Not always, of course, but

9

Rags to Riches

in the tiredness of so many of our present structures we are led to this way of thinking and acting, however unconsciously.

It may be better for us, too, to build a new house rather than spend too much time and money on the old ones.

My confrère, Henri le Boursicaud, has written the story of a remarkable group of people who live and see the gospel in a new way. There was little for my personal comfort in this book, quite the opposite.

May some person, braver than I, who reads this book have the courage to start a community of the Companions of Emmaus in Ireland. I think that would greatly please Henri, and his friend Jacques, who prefer to live in idealism rather than die indifferent.

Raphael Gallagher CSsR
27 May 1991

Introduction

In January 1978, I wrote to about a hundred friends: Today, I have just had the idea of starting a joint project to ''tell'' what the Emmaus communities are.

I have written about ten short chapters in response to questions such as:

What is Emmaus?

How did Emmaus begin?

How does it work?

Who controls the communities?

What do you do, exactly?

Where do you live?

What is it like to live in your communities?

Is it true that you never drink alcohol?

Where do you stand in today's world?

And, of course:

Where does the future of Emmaus lie?

What I am asking you to do is to read each chapter and to jot down, in the wide margin, anything which you think might add to the text — a reflection which adds to it, an event illustrating a point, an enriching viewpoint, a constructive criticism or even a thought-provoking question.'

There are already several books about Emmaus. They are classical, serious and interesting. A film called simply *Les Chiffoniers d'Emmaus* has been made. There have also been newspaper articles and television debates to inform and educate the public about Emmaus. However, there are still many people who question us about the basics of the movement. Only the other day, a forty-three-year-old engineer wrote to me, asking:

How long has Emmaus been in existence?

What is the movement's aim?

How does it function?

Have the results to date been in accordance with the original aim? Other frequent questions are:

Does Abbé Pierre remain the true leader of the communities?

What is the lifestyle of the Companions?

In response to letters or telephone calls, we go to all types of homes. Recently, one of our visits was to the home of a science lecturer where we were given no mean welcome. His cry of 'Good luck' was warm and heartfelt. I would have liked to have offered him a copy of this book.

When Michel, a young man in search of meaning in life, questioned us about Emmaus I wished even more for a copy of this book to explain our way of life, and perhaps to offer him the answer he sought.

I am frequently touched by the generosity of old people, who are perhaps retiring and moving house for the last time. They open their homes to us, offering us their precious souvenirs and keepsakes. Why should we not offer them something in exchange, a souvenir that may warm their hearts?

Once a month I meet an old priest who is in ill-health and who passionately wants to understand Emmaus more fully. I invite you to read this, Father. This is Emmaus, such as we are.

Over the past seven years, the Companions here at Charenton have been in at least five thousand houses, using just our single removal van. It seems fitting that these few pages should go to show that we are not simply arms that collect goods, but that we also have a face and a heart.

I would also like to present this book to a certain fat gentleman who tried to persuade us to clean out his cellar, packed with useless junk, *free of charge*, for the sole reason that 'Your aim is to serve, is it not?' It is true that we wish to serve others. But not those who are already rich enough to pay their own servants. We will willingly leave him this book *free of charge* to correct his idea of Emmaus.

Our community, like all Emmaus communities, runs a little bric-à-brac shop selling all kinds of odds and ends. People come and go seeking bargains and inexpensive treasures. I see in this little book an opportunity to present our story, with the other second-hand paperbacks on sale in the corridor or in some convenient little corner.

Do these bargain-hunting visitors seek only a cheap armchair, a pair of slippers or a bedside lamp? One of the first questions Christ put to his earliest disciples was, 'What are you looking for?' Part of all authentic humanity is this curiosity, this searching which is unaware of the depths of its desire. 'I am looking for...a word to show me the way.' Who knows whether we may find in all this bric-à-brac a page of the Gospel written today. Hundreds, even thousands of people of all ages and backgrounds come and go at Emmaus, forever searching. Could not an easily read book, unpretentious and full of life, cause the spark to blaze up for those who are secretly looking for a light? 'I have come to bring light to the world.'

Perhaps I am full of ideals and illusions, but in writing this book I have not forgotten my Companions, the Emmaus workers, those of the present and those of the future. Who knows, perhaps some of them will become more aware of their reasons for continuing along the Emmaus road, the road of freedom and hope, and therefore stronger in their resolve to do so.

One of my fellow workers here who suffers from insomnia

read these pages in two nights, in the nocturnal silence that is conducive to thought. What was his verdict?

His exact words were: 'I find these chapters, which will become a book, perfectly written. Above all, they allow one to understand more distinctly the reason for our work. They encourage us to continue with enthusiasm.'

'To continue'? These chapters may encourage you to begin. Who knows, perhaps there is a place for you among the Companions of Emmaus in the service of those who have experienced great suffering.

Henri Le Boursicaud

Prologue

'Yes, André, that's it', I said.

André sized up the courthouse with a look. He didn't utter a single word but his face became more serious. Since we left Paris this morning we have covered almost 400 kilometres together, practically without speaking. André is certainly the strong, silent type.

At midday we had lunch on the banks of the Loire. Sitting on the dry grass, sheltered by an embankment, he did pass a comment. 'It's nice here' he remarked. The deep silence of the countryside swallowed up his words in an instant.

It's true that our simple but deep friendship puts us at ease together. Seated beneath the weak rays of the October sun our hearts are as one. We are brothers, two Companions of Emmaus....

We are early: there are certain meetings for which it is better to be on time! I suggest to André that we pass the time by exploring this pleasant country town, but he prefers to wait here. He is thinking — nervous perhaps, even though he does not show it. In any case, why is he afraid? He has done nothing wrong. Summoned to attend, he didn't *want* to appear before the circuit court.

André is a good Companion of Emmaus. He has spent the past fifteen years working here and there around the country. Living in one or other of the eighty-five communities, he practises his trade of dismantling old cookers and fridges. Being popular with the others and a

15

conscientious worker, he is sure of a warm welcome wherever he goes.

For fifteen years he has done nothing but work for those less fortunate than himself. He is not alone in this — the Companions in France alone number two thousand. His comrades know only that he has suffered cruelly: nobody knows the full story since he never speaks of his past and is not questioned about it. In fifteen years he has earned tens of thousands of pounds, simply by dismantling and renovating other people's junk. Like all the Companions, he keeps only a tiny sum for his own pocket-money and has discreetly given away almost all of his earnings. His one love is the countryside, with its tranquillity and peace. André is a hermit at heart, often working for three or four months without letting up and then taking to the road, to find peace and rest in solitude.

A while ago he nodded towards one of the natural caves which are common on hillsides in this part of the country. He spoke pensively, as if to himself: 'I lived there for a few months once. I used to eat well — some salt, a few potatoes, oil and vinegar, water to drink and left-over meat that was sold as dog-food. Didn't cost me much for a meal! With the little I earned from selling wild fruit or any pieces of leather or odds and ends I found buried in rubbish bins, I couldn't afford to spend wildly. At night, covered by an overcoat, I slept soundly.'

I drank in every word he uttered. This man was one of my fellow-workers, but I knew he would always be a wanderer at heart. For years now, his only form of relaxation has been to move on, to roam at will from one Emmaus community to another. It was a rare privilege to hear any details of these journeys.

*   *   *

On several occasions the police didn't take his rambling as casually as he appeared to. 'No identification, no money, no fixed abode.... This is a very serious matter', the solemn voice of the law would intone. André sees no crime in this and doesn't feel obliged to defend himself. In his eyes, liberty is a basic human right. Unconcerned, he goes on his own sweet way. After all he sees both his fellow human beings and the countryside he inhabits as his good friends. These solitary journeys are vital to nourish that friendship, to maintain his humanity, the quality of his life and his peace of mind.

The police don't take things so lightly. They write bulky reports on people like André, as if they were serious criminals. Files fill up with reports about André in police offices. Information flows in, but this carefree tramp remains elusive.

This time, however, he has been caught and is threatened with imprisonment. It is time to play their game, take this seriously, go to court and explain himself once and for all.... He is finally taking his friends' advice. Eight hundred thousand others are homeless wanderers like him. In Paris alone, twenty-five thousand people live without a home. (Might we ask whose fault this is?) He just sleeps rough when he is passing through an area, simply moving around to unwind, to take a holiday and get back to basics. Holidays are fashionable nowadays, after all. André wants to remain human, not to become a beast of burden!

As we were early, I naively decided to look to the local parish priest for support. We were in a large, wealthy parish and I found the representative of Our Lord behind a desk covered with weighty books and reports. His response to my request was discouraging: 'No, I know absolutely nobody at the court who could help him.' Keeping his eyes on the paper-weight on his desk, he added coldly, 'The law must be respected.'

Deep in thought, I return through the winding streets to the court-house. Workers are erecting scaffolding around it — apparently they are spending a few thousand to give it a face-lift, to reinforce its air of authority.

André is waiting inside, standing in the hall, his posture stooped, as if defeated by the might of the law. Lawyers begin to arrive for the afternoon hearings. They are totally at ease here, laughing and smiling, their cheeks reddened after a relaxing lunch washed down by a bottle of good wine. They shake hands and greet each other enthusiastically. Their confident voices fill the hall where a few young people wait for the afternoon's proceedings to begin. Some standing, some sitting, they are tight-lipped and nervous. One of them is handcuffed and accompanied by two policemen. At 2.30 exactly the great doors open wide. We trail in. I saw a large crucifix somewhere (or did I dream it afterwards?). It is not so long since the parish priest used to preside at the opening.

I can think only of Christ, silent before Pilate.

*   *   *

On the rostrum, there are two men and a woman, all quite young; on the right, a man whom I think must be the state prosecutor. A cocoon-like silence descends. The occasion must be serious and impressive for all of us.

I am sitting at the back on a plain wooden bench. I wait, turning my cap nervously in my hands. I don't have to wait for very long. André is one of the first to be called and he plants himself squarely in the middle of the floor, directly before the rostrum, like a schoolboy who must explain himself to the headmaster. The charge against him is read aloud, complete with a full list of dates and locations. It is

18

a list of chance meetings between this traveller and the police. After a few moments of silence, the judges whisper conspiratorially together and sentence is passed.

I can't have heard correctly! Two weeks in prison for taking a holiday! I am horrified.

Confident of his answers, the judge questions André. 'Do you have anything to say?...'(silence). 'No fixed abode?...'(silence). 'No intention of finding a home?...'

Before he has finished' speaking I am on my feet, exclaiming: 'Excuse me, gentlemen! André lives and works in an Emmaus community.' Every policeman present shoots me down with a look — but nobody dares to throw me out for having spoken out of turn during an act of this rural theatre.

'Who are *you*?' A voice from the rostrum is raised in reproach. I am not thrown by this, quite the opposite. I reply, confident of André's innocence and of the justice of the cause I am defending — the right to freedom, 'André is, like me, a Companion of Emmaus.' Quizzical looks from all sides — I can read their minds: 'Emmaus? What's that?'

And so I pleaded my case, I explained, I spoke of.... Of what *did* I speak? I told them of the truth of Emmaus, its inspiration, its direction, its mystique...in short, what I wish to explain in this book.

My speech for the defence did not fall on deaf ears. All charges against André were dropped!

1

We are not beggars

'What is Emmaus?'

When we are called, by phone or letter, to come and get what other people no longer want, we like to set to work immediately. We do not like to spend time on lengthy explanations, even though we are frequently received with a mixture of hospitality and curiosity. To avoid this we give people a letter like the following:

> I wish to thank you on behalf of the Emmaus-Liberty community at Charenton for your invitation.
>
> The Emmaus movement has almost one hundred houses in five continents and was founded by Abbé Pierre, who, at the age of seventy-seven, still leads this large family.
>
> Emmaus began in the spring of 1949, when Abbé Pierre, a former member of parliament, met a man who had tried to kill himself. Instead of seeking a reason for his despair, Abbé Pierre asked this man for help. Greatly influenced by this friendly request, the man's despair faded away and his will to live was renewed. He often claimed afterwards: 'It was not *things* that I lacked, but a reason to live'. Abbé Pierre's request instantly gave him a meaning in life: 'Help me to do something for those less fortunate than us. I can't manage to do it all alone....'
>
> With the meeting of these two people, the first

Emmaus community was born. Ever since, thousands of men and women have heard the same request and have given their lives to answering it in whatever part of the world they live. These are the Companions of Emmaus.

Joining Emmaus means reversing one's values. Personal profit, which most people seek first, must take second place. Humanity must come first, the service of the needy must take precedence: we can then create a new Person in a new World.

The Emmaus workers live and eat together and each person makes do with just £5 for himself. The extra money that we earn is given to those who need it, in whichever country they may be. There is nothing heroic in this — but neither is it easy.

You have contacted us and have received our reply. Once again, many thanks for your kind offer. May this brief encounter deepen our understanding of one another.

Most people are touched by our story and invite us to their homes, offering us anything from papers to clothes to scrap metal to old furniture, books, trinkets, and machines of all types. One old lady even gave her gold wedding ring, wishing to be a part of this generous work. Love lives on in every human heart.

Thanks to such people, Emmaus has grown and spread throughout the world, and money has been earned for those who need it.

Not all are so generous, however. We occasionally get calls from people who seek only to take advantage of us. They want to give us useless junk that they cannot get rid of — in effect, to have us clean out their cellars for free! Instead of helping the poor, these people exploit them. We trust this is not your intention.

As you have contacted us in order to help the poor,

we hope you understand what Abbé Pierre is continually teaching — that it is dishonest to seek to help the poor without attacking the causes of poverty and social injustice, whatever they may be. If we are truly to work together as Companions against poverty, we must go this far. Otherwise we are simply mindless fools who are being exploited — and you, by doing nothing more than giving to a 'good cause', are just hypocrites who hide behind charity to avoid the issue of justice.

It is clearly impossible to explain ourselves and our mission to you fully in such a short visit. If you wish to know more, Abbé Pierre compiles a magazine, *Faims et Soifs des Hommes*, which is available from 2 Avenue de la liberté, Charenton-le-Pont, France. This will inform and enlighten you on the issues with which we struggle, and will enable you to act more effectively against poverty.

Yours,
The Companions of Emmaus

At Emmaus we are not beggars. Our trade is complex and varied. Even a brief synopsis of our work will take up several pages. We are rag-and-bone workers or, rather, recyclers — first and foremost a *team* whose trade is retrieving rubbish. Because of the nature of our work, each community is a veritable hive of activity.

The whole process begins with the collection. Sometimes it's a big clear-out: a few of us arrive in an area or a town, hold meetings, put up posters and announce our imminent arrival, explaining who we are. Then we invade *en masse* with our jeeps or lorries and relieve the townspeople of whatever surplus goods they wish to dispose of.

Alternatively, generally in the Paris area, individuals may

contact us for a private collection. We simply arrange a date and time and turn up at their houses. Afterwards the varied and interesting objects we have collected are sorted, cleaned, repaired and sold. It's a simple process, which is its great attraction for the Emmaus workers. Literally anyone will find a niche in the large range of jobs involved in recycling.

Everything must be sorted properly and listed; clothes (according to type of garment), iron, non-ferrous metals; the furniture must be sent for repair, the chairs to be re-upholstered, the motors, televisions, radios and bicycles to be fixed.... Mechanics, drivers, furniture-makers, masons, cooks, plumbers and gardeners are especially welcome at Emmaus, but due to the nature of our work even an unskilled worker invariably finds a place in the process.

This is one of the most important principles of Emmaus. Anybody who knocks on our door is welcomed. We give every new arrival a good meal, make them welcome and find them a place to sleep. Each person is treated as a new friend — we don't ask whether they are 'viable' or 'qualified' to work with us.

It could happen one day that an Emmaus leader would become over-anxious to run a profitable business, placing too much emphasis on achieving high productivity. Then joining Emmaus would be no different from finding any other job — the applicant would be assessed according to demanding criteria, judged on age, physical build, address.... People would be employed or turned away depending on their 'worth'. The spirit of Emmaus would be irretrievably lost. This never happens at Emmaus — and it is worth reiterating that it never must!

*   *   *

Will our trade ever leave us redundant? In a consumer society such as ours there will always be a place for those who recycle waste. Many people use goods and don't know how to dispose of them afterwards. Rich and poor alike hoard useless objects and remnants in attics, spare rooms, apartments, basements....

Once, after the death of the resident of a tiny two-roomed apartment we were called in and filled three jeeps to overflowing with the rubbish that had been collected there! I could barely get one foot inside the bathroom door; the room was chock-a-block with countless boxes of string carrying the strange label, 'In Case of War'!

So many people say 'One of these days we must clear the place out', but usually this occurs only when the occupant dies or moves house. The rich seem to gather up even more, keeping things in their own, their children's or even their parents' homes. 'One of these days it could come in handy, you never know....' (Usually it ends up rotting in somebody's cellar.) In the end, space runs out and people are forced to look for help. 'Why not call the Companions of Emmaus, they seem to do a good job?'

Then we are contacted, by phone or letter. We have a book in which we note the day and time arranged. From then on anything can happen. I could write a book about the surprises that have awaited us at our numerous destinations. We take what we are offered — from pieces of cardboard, to books, to clothes, old rags, newspapers, and all sorts of knick-knacks. Normally, three of us set out in a jeep or lorry on the day in question. Each house has one or two vehicles, the larger houses having three or four.

The collection is often very hard work — carrying old cookers down narrow stairs from a fifth or sixth floor apartment, sometimes moving heavy old pianos into the lorry. In a loaded van or lorry returning from a day's collecting you will find literally everything but the kitchen sink — and often even that as well! Clean or dirty dishes, chairs, armchairs, sofas, beds, mattresses, canopies, sideboards, wardrobes (the ones that can be dismantled are easy!), bags of newspapers, rags, clothes, coal.... As you can see we're not fussy once we are offered things that can be used again.

Most people who contact us really want to help. They are welcoming, reasonable in what they offer us and don't try to force us to take away useless items. Others take us for rubbish collectors, telling us 'You're taking the good things, take the bad with them.' We balk at this, obviously. We try to explain ourselves, 'What do you expect us to do with a dirty, torn, smelly old mattress?' but some even have the nerve to retort, 'Well you are there to provide a service, aren't you?' We are forced to make our position clear: 'We are there to serve others, yes, but not to serve just anybody. The rich already have too many servants!' One day, in order to 'serve others' we were expected to clear out four cellars packed with rotting wood that had been gathered during the First World War! Faced with such immorality and exploitation we have to take the hard line: 'Either you pay us for our work or you go elsewhere.'

Then there are those, especially the very rich, who have absolutely no idea of the price of things. For example, one afternoon we were called upon to collect some paper — nothing else but paper. On our arrival we found about one hundred kilos of various magazines in a garage. The owner had obviously not thought about it: one hundred kilos at 1p for every two kilos comes to £5 (this was in 1976). When you take into account the journey we made, the price of the petrol, and our time, we lost money on this. The old lady couldn't see our point and would not give in. She even got angry and declared in a peremptory tone 'That's what your organisation is for.' This lady was wrong. We are not there to be exploited but to help those less fortunate than ourselves. That is our true aim.

Usually we don't have this problem. Most people who

call us mean well. Sometimes, thinking aloud, they can be unwittingly cruel — 'Yes, Marie, give them that, it's no use to anybody any more.' They give to rid themselves of junk but also to help the Companions of Emmaus.

On our return home, at no matter what hour of day or night, everything is quickly unloaded. All the metal in one corner, furniture in the other, papers, boxes and clothes are sorted and put to one side. Next day the jeep or lorry sets out again and a fascinating amount of activity gets under way at the house.

Let's look at the various jobs undertaken. First comes the 'demolisher'. Winter or summer he is to be seen at work in the open air, attacking an old cooker or fridge. (Those that can be used are kept to one side.) Working with a sledgehammer and screwdriver he literally rips them apart. The cast-iron goes in one corner, the flexes and wiring go together, the copper somewhere else.... It takes quite a bit of patience but he keeps at it doggedly to recuperate a little non-ferrous metal.

Another worker is re-seating chairs. He begins by stabilising the back and legs, then spends hours weaving the cane in and out. Finally he straightens up and examines his work critically. He is happy, it is a job well done.

The cook also puts in a hard day's work. In a house with up to forty Companions, he has to rise early and can't afford to waste time.

Next comes the laundry-worker. Everybody has to have clothes washed and ironed and ready to wear for Saturday evening.

Then there is the carpenter. He spends his time working on wardrobes, tables and furniture, some of which need quite a bit of repair — but what satisfaction he gets from a job well done when he sees his polished and varnished furniture shining so brilliantly afterwards!

Here and there, in huge hangars, there are workers with

electric or hand presses; they are making large balls, weighing one or two hundred kilos, with paper, cloth or boxes. Each ball is carefully sealed with iron rings and they are piled neatly together before being taken away in lorry-loads of twenty or thirty tonnes. These workers are placid and easygoing: some of them have been doing the same work for years, sure in the knowledge that their job is just as important as that of a driver or community leader, or even of the founders of Emmaus.

Let us not forget the work of the gardener. Where there is enough space one of the members looks after a vegetable garden. What a pleasure it is to have fresh leeks and tomatoes; the gardener may rightly be proud of them.

We haven't mentioned the salesman, who has a nerve-racking job, or the telephonist, always talking to someone. In the larger houses these are two important jobs.

Then we need somebody to welcome visitors. So many Companions come to the door that somebody must always be available to prepare the rooms, welcome newcomers and show them where to start work. A former accountant won't necessarily know how to make bales of cardboard and must be taught — and it is often more difficult to teach the newcomer than actually to do the work.

The different jobs to be done vary from country to country. In Rwanda, in central Africa, an Emmaus group makes transistors and clothes. Are they simply a business, then, just like any other factory? Yet these workers bring handicapped children out of the jungle, especially polio victims, and give them hospital care, an education and a trade — something which is invaluable in Africa — so that one day they will be able to return to their families and live on their earnings. What's more, twenty-six of them have cleared over ten thousand square metres of jungle and grow potatoes, sweet potatoes, cabbage, red cabbage, aubergines, onions, leeks, lettuce, tomatoes, cauliflower, chicory and

27

carrots. They support 1,544 colleagues. They made thousands of bricks themselves and built their own house. They are learning to make tables, chairs and beds from salvaged materials.

In Nigeria another community has also undertaken an agricultural enterprise. For this purpose they bring together poor workers with no qualifications and unemployed graduates. Elsewhere in Africa, Emmaus workers have set up a small tannery. In the Indies they have taken up fishing. In Latin America, workshops have developed around dumping grounds for old cars: these have become ideal centres for training apprentices in car mechanics. All it took was somebody to come up with the idea. In Chile, another Emmaus group has opened a hostel to house the Indians who come down from the Andes looking for work.

The specific activities vary from one country to another, but the essence of the movement never varies — we come to the aid of those who have less than we do. The French communities generally work at recycling, but it must be emphasised that any work is suitable for Emmaus. The essential factor is that all money earned must be divided in three parts. One third is used to cover all the living expenses of the companions, another third to found new communities, and a third is given to those in need.

In France, some women in the Emmaus movement have begun to make mattresses, preparing and grading the cloth used. Some are learning furniture restoration while others run a boutique dealing in both modern and twenties-style clothes.

Formerly, groups of workers were known as the 'Emmaus builders'. Their mission was to travel from place to place building homes for those who needed them. Even today, the companions usually build or convert their own houses, and any other buildings needed for their work.

When the movement first began, the pioneers started to

recycle rubbish. This work is still carried on at some centres, and for some communities, it is still the main source of income. It is not, however, essential to the spirit of Emmaus. Even in the developed countries a community could quite easily specialise in agriculture. This might cause a few problems, but there is no good reason why it should not be done. The only obligation would be that the work should not be done for profit alone. The spirit of Emmaus is kept alive once the community does not work to become rich. Usually, a community will need about one third of its profits for day-to-day living. Everything over and above that must be given away.

Having said this, the work of recycling still prospers in France. It even looks as though it may be about to improve further, with the rising cost of raw materials. Yves and Françoise, a young couple who are leaders of the Poitiers community in the West of France, have this to say: 'Our task of recycling waste material is now taking on a new aspect, that of combatting unnecessary waste. The Emmaus workers didn't wait to be told to combat what is a scandal in the eyes of two-thirds of the world's population. In just one year, and with minimal resources, our community has ploughed over seven hundred tonnes of raw materials back into the economy.'

The Companions in Lyons provide us with figures for their achievements. 'In 1974 we collected:
— 47 tonnes of cloth,
— 261 tonnes of cardboard and paper,
— 55 tonnes of iron and raw materials.'
Each of the Emmaus houses could cite such statistics.

Need I say that Emmaus has no place for 'hangers on'. Like everywhere else, we do come across a few lazybones. Layabouts, thieves and traitors try to mingle in the ranks of all organisations and classes, but anybody who stays in Emmaus is anything but lazy. It is impossible to get away with twiddling your thumbs for long. Very soon, the idle person is rooted out and given an ultimatum: 'Either pull your weight or leave.' One of the Companions expresses this perfectly: 'Anybody who comes to Emmaus with the intention of living at the community's expense and taking advantage of the others will automatically be thrown out.'

A community leader declares: 'The work here is hard and demanding. The Companions make do with very little, just a few pounds each week. Even though they have their food and a home, it's still not much money — but under no circumstances will any of these people accept charity. They insist on working honestly to earn their living.' An Emmaus community is certainly not a safe haven from the real world.

This is true even of the older Companions who have retired and live in a special Emmaus house near Rouen. Various types of workshops give them the opportunity to live life to the full as they work, each according to his or her ability, in the autumn of their lives. It is not always easy to lead such a community: yet the Companions continue to work, earning dignity and a meaning in life which prevents them slipping into bourgeois, egoistic attitudes. It is a case of work being made for the people and not people for the work.

*　　*　　*

Often when Companions arrive at our door they are exhausted from days spent walking or nights of sleeping rough. They are welcomed, allowed to sleep and rest for a few days. This is only natural, and everybody understands the situation. But it cannot go on indefinitely. Once new arrivals have recovered they must become part of the community and pull their weight.

We all get up at a set time every morning — usually around 7.00 a.m. In the bigger houses, everybody is woken by a bell or gong. In the smaller communities, however, things are more easygoing, the only rule being, for the early risers, not to wake the others, and for the sleepy-heads, to be up by 8.00 at the latest. We work an eight- or nine-hour day, taking Sunday off. There are some who even potter around and work a little on Sunday also.

We don't work an extraordinary amount, just the same as anybody else. The difference is in our *attitude* to work. We are proud to work. As *Emmaüs-Flash*, one of our bulletins in France, said: 'For us, here at Emmaus, our work gives us the right to live as we wish, it is our freedom.' Work means being able to eat with the pride of the honest worker who has earned his bread. It means the pride of having a little extra to share with those who need it.

We work together in order to be able to share — to share amongst ourselves and to share with others who knock on our door. Abbé Pierre emphasises this: 'The Companions of Emmaus are the ragpickers and recyclers of our wasteful society (even though they are too frequently looked upon as garbage collectors). That is how the public sees them. But each of these individuals is basically part of a community. They have chosen to live together with the common aim of helping those less well off than themselves.'

We do realise that we can do very little in relation to the size of the problem. One community put it like this: 'We are all well aware that anything we can do will be just a drop in the ocean of work that must be done to bring about justice, and thereby peace, in the world.' Lucie Coutaz, who has worked with Abbé Pierre since the foundation of Emmaus, notes however: 'On looking at the Emmaus movement from outside, one is struck by the huge amount that has been achieved with such small resources.'

We are not beggars, but we are agitators, prophets who shock people out of their set ways of thinking and acting, who provoke and incite a revolution in attitudes. 'In short', says Abbé Pierre, 'Emmaus houses are communities of poor people, workers who welcome anybody who turns up to work with them, without looking for profit. Their sole aim is to lead a dignified life, to be able to work and to earn enough to allow them to give plenty away and to say to those who lack nothing: 'See what we have achieved with what you leave after you. If you, who have both financial assets and political power, were to try to equal this, would not many of the world's problems be solved?'

2

They have suffered...

At this stage, you will no doubt wonder about many of the practical questions raised by our set-up. One of the most important of these, and invariably the first one we are asked, is: 'What kind of people join these communities? Where do you find members?'

The answer is simple — ninety-nine per cent of us are people who have suffered. We are the injured of the world, suffering either physically or emotionally.

Some of the Companions have never known their parents. The childhood of an orphan is lonely and hard, and one needs to be very lucky in life in order to recover from it. There are others who enjoyed a wonderful family life for years until it was shattered by the death of a spouse, divorce, war or bankruptcy, and their lives fell apart. Others married and, full of hope and dreams, set up a home only to see themselves hurt and their homes destroyed. Some were even separated from their children. Thus practically all of the Companions have loved and lost in some way, and have been devastated by this separation.

Many of the Companions, especially those aged between thirty-five and fifty, have been hardworking employees for years, often in dangerous and stressful trades. No statistics have been established, but an extraordinarily large percentage of our members have been seriously injured, either during the course of their work or by war.

We all work energetically and eat heartily, but, more so

Rags to Riches

than in other milieux, most of us appear old for our years. Abused by the world, physically and emotionally, our health and our appearance tell the tale, and for many of us alcoholism has aggravated our condition.

Even worse than the loss of our health, many of the Companions have lost all dignity. They were made to feel like objects rather than people. They have been trampled on by a society whose only value is money, money to be earned by any means, even by the exploitation of the disadvantaged. The owner of a small family-run business once admitted frankly to me that he himself was obliged 'continually to trample on his heart' in order to keep his business on the road.

It is shattering for a worker to feel for years upon end that he is no more than one of his employer's possessions, that the machine he operates is treated with more respect than he is. When unemployment is widespread workers are easily replaced. This costs the employer nothing and may even benefit him. Nowadays however, even a slightly complicated machine is very expensive. When workers observe, throughout their entire working life, that the machine gets better treatment than the workforce, then they will certainly have a chip on their shoulder. It makes us wonder about the kind of world, the kind of hell, we live in.

And you ask who are the Companions of Emmaus? Many of them are the bruised hearts, the battered bodies and the bewildered souls of our society. Take, for example the story of Hyacinthe — a story that is typical of so many others.

*   *   *

Hyacinthe had been with us for a month when, one morning, he drank a little too much. I watched him staggering around and maybe he realised that I understood him. He went for a lie down on his bed.

34

When evening came and he had slept it off, he decided to leave us. He wanted to leave that very night, right in the middle of winter, although he didn't know yet which direction he would take. North or south? It depended on his mood when he got to the nearest Metro station.... It didn't really matter to him anyway.

Sitting opposite each other, we spoke a little. He was conscious of the fact that he had worked for an entire month for people who were suffering more than him. Though he had said practically nothing during that month, he began to confide in me. 'Abbé Pierre did a wonderful thing by setting up Emmaus', he said. He now wanted to leave, probably in the hope of turning over a new leaf and starting all over again.

Perhaps sensing that I understood, he continued in a monotone: 'I never knew my mother, she died at twenty. As for my father — never knew him either! At twelve years of age I was working on a farm in Aisne. For dinner I always ate bacon — with some dandelions I used to collect in the fields. The owners pretended to eat with me but afterwards I was sent out to the yard to do a few odd jobs and I would hear the clatter of plates as the table was set so that they could have a proper meal. What a way to treat a twelve-year-old! I was hurt and hungry but I said nothing. From time to time, the local priest would visit all the housewives in turn. This seemed like a good way of getting to know his parishioners but you must admit that it was also a handy way of getting free meals! On this particular day, everyone was gathered around the priest at the family dinner-table, which, of course, was piled high with food. That certainly made a change from bacon and dandelions! Each of them would cast a stealthy glance at me in turn, when they got a chance, as I was eating heartily. Once the woman of the house remarked on it. ''He has a good appetite, he eats well.'' '

That did it! Hyacinthe couldn't control himself any longer. He looked up from his plate and replied insolently: 'You old cow! The priest has to come to your house so that I can have a decent meal. Every other day I get only bacon and dandelions!'

The family said nothing.... Better just to smile indulgently and give the impression that the 'poor servant boy' isn't quite normal....

The following day, however, Hyacinthe was beaten and sent on his way. For years he worked at different jobs on other farms, just making enough to feed himself. At twenty-five he signed up and went off to the war. After five years he came back and worked with the threshing machine, going from one farm to another all year round. As he said himself, 'Those were the days!'

One evening, four years ago, he was walking along the road when a motorist knocked him down and then sped off. A few days later his leg had to be amputated.

And that's it, his story...

* * *

We shook hands. He stood up, ready to leave.... What a life he had had! Hyacinthe, where are you today? In which community? On what road?

I told this story to Emmanuel, a Portuguese immigrant who had been a Companion of Emmaus for three years. He listened for a little while, then without letting me finish he broke in. 'But that's just like my life story! I was the same, at twelve years of age...'

Usually a Companion of Emmaus will tell very little of his past. It is rare to have somebody confide in you as Hyacinthe did. And who would dare to question them? Who would risk stirring up a painful memory, rubbing salt in wounds that are still open? Friends will hear the story in bits and pieces. For instance, one of the Companions once said to me, 'At fourteen I was a runaway slave.' Just that, not another word. His face told enough of the story.

*   *   *

A friend of mine once protested that Emmaus was merely putting all the poor together and not solving any problems. 'But', I asked him, 'if these were handicapped or injured people, would you not say that they could understand each other best and could therefore help each other?' 'You make too much of a big deal about being a "community"', he retorted. 'It's all just a big farce, you're really just a work group.'

At Emmaus it would take somebody who has not suffered like Hyacinthe forever to understand, or even recognise, the simple but sincere gestures that form a community among us. Perhaps our society, with all its formalities and boundaries would do well to learn to live a little like this.

It is difficult to realise the meaning of a clear smile, a warm handshake, a friendly 'hello', an affectionate 'how are things'.... When a friend who rarely speaks says out of the blue: 'I really feel that I'm loved here' and surprises even himself at his ability to express his feelings, it is hard to discount the value of living in community.

Real friendship is not looking into each other's eyes but looking forward together towards a single goal. True companionship among those who have suffered consists not in speaking of each other's pain but in working shoulder-to-shoulder to help those who have suffered even more.

By now you are probably saying: 'This is all talk, nothing more than fine words....' Read the testimony of a Companion, written after spending two years at Emmaus. Then judge for yourself.

Charenton, France
23 November 1977

Thoughts and Reflections on Emmaus

Having spent almost two years with the Emmaus community in Charenton, I have decided to write a few words about the way of life here, what it's like to live in a community and how people from outside see us. These are the things that have struck me most forcibly.

Firstly, when somebody joins a community, he is immediately well received and feels himself surrounded by friendship and love. This often counts for much more than any other organisation can offer.

To secure their happiness and give their lives meaning, it is vital for everyone to have a goal in life. Ours is to serve those who have need of us, and by our work we feel we can help others to get back on their feet and regain their dignity. The Companions of Emmaus could also be called Companions of liberty, since without this freedom we would be nothing. The worthwhile feeling in a community is the friendship between us and the joy of working towards a goal, instead of striving for something that is worthless. In the 'normal' world people work for a boss, often one who exploits them. It is sad to see the middle classes living so well on money that others have worked for. By our work, we show that we have our two feet planted more firmly on the ground than many of these people.

A few months later the author of these lines was elected by his friends to become leader of a community of forty Companions. Today he is married and continues to lead his community with the same vitality.

When two Portuguese women and a man visited the Emmaus communities in France, with a view to founding Emmaus-Liberty in their own country, I gave them some advice: 'As you observe the French communities, take note of what *not* to do in Portugal.'

Should some Irish people decide to found Emmaus fraternities in their country, I would give them the same advice. I think that they would soon notice that the greatest joy exists wherever there is most sharing and most struggle for justice.

3

The three beginnings of Emmaus

The other day, a friendly caretaker said to me: 'I always thought Emmaus began with M.' I had to laugh, thinking of the shaky beginnings of Emmaus, as its pioneers struggled to spread the movement.

Who recruited the original members? The state? The government?... It is true that the police busy themselves with tramps and beggars on the streets. They round them up every night, but only to move them on out of the way. Their efforts at improving these 'human debris' have been ineffective to say the least....

The trade unions, perhaps? A friend of mine who is a trade union leader confided in me: 'Henri, my friend, we can't manage them....' He seemed thoughtful, even unhappy about it. He shrugged his shoulders and sighed deeply: 'What can we do? We can't be everywhere. Our job is to unite the largest possible number of workers from the factories and production lines, to recruit and inspire future trade union members.... You understand how it is?'

Yes, my friend, I understand. Those who have no work and no hope must take second place once again.

Was it the Church then, directing her attention to the poor? Numerous episcopal and papal declarations on poverty, together with those of the Vatican Council, have filled volumes of books and magazines. But the hierarchical

Church is still a Church *for* the poor rather than one *of* the poor. It is still not a Church of *total* sharing. Events in Brazil and elsewhere serve to accentuate the gap between the poor and some Vatican officials. As I said to one Portuguese bishop who asked me what I thought of his people, 'The people are close to God — but the Church is far from them'.

Another friend of mine was under the impression that 'Emmaus' was a famous man who led our communities. There is, in fact a 'Mr Emmaus' who leads us, a well-known French politician known to us as Abbé Pierre — a 'big shot' with a big heart.

In the early days there were, in a manner of speaking, three births of Emmaus, three separate times when groups of Companions gathered together, eventually becoming the first three communities. Each time Abbé Pierre was there, but he was not alone... When speaking of it himself he always uses the plural: 'It wasn't an initiative from the Paris community which started it, rather everything was due to the spontaneous efforts we made when we felt it necessary on the spot.' He always holds that nothing was according to plan, nothing was programmed to happen. Life simply produced these events. 'Emmaus is not something that my friends and I *did*; it just *happened* to us.'

First birth: Meeting George

Father Henri-Antoine Grouès, a curate in Grenoble in 1942, found himself chaplain to the navy after the war. From his involvement in the underground resistance, he took on the codename of one of his comrades, Pierre, and became known as 'Abbé Pierre'.

He was elected a representative for the Nancy area and while looking for a house in Paris, decided to rent one of the abandoned properties in the suburbs. A friend of his who worked with the poor of the city suggested that he allow poor families from the inner city to spend weekends in this large suburban house.

After the bombings and destruction of the war, there was an acute shortage of housing in the Parisian region. Abbé Pierre's mansion could have housed two large families comfortably. The idea sparked his imagination. He decided to call his house the 'Emmaus House'. Emmaus was the name of the village where a house of refuge opened the eyes of the discouraged disciples who had met a stranger on the road, allowing them to regain their enthusiasm and recognise their Companion in the breaking of the bread. The stranger was Jesus.

Emmaus became a place of refuge at the end of the line, a place for those who had despaired, who had hit rock bottom, a house of encouragement and resurrection. Abbé Pierre didn't realise how apt his choice of name was to become.

In the summer of 1949, Abbé Pierre was on his way back from Stockholm where he had just been elected to the executive committee of the World Federalist Movement, when he received an urgent call to help a friend of his. George was a former convict who had just come out of prison having served twenty years. He had been sentenced to life imprisonment but had been released on good behaviour.

The poor man had returned home to find, instead of a joyful reunion, a family in which there was no longer any room for him. His wife was living with another man and had given birth to a child. Emotionally scarred by an injustice perpetrated against him many years previously, George lost all hope and tried to kill himself.

Abbé Pierre came to the aid of his suicidal friend. He could have offered him money, a home, a job.... Being a high-ranking member of the government, he would have had little trouble obtaining anything George asked him for.

Instead, he offered him nothing but compassion. Compassion means letting the pain of another enter your heart, so that you can say with sincerity, 'I want to struggle with you to heal your pain, which has become mine'. What Abbé Pierre did say to George was, 'You are obviously free and have no obligations. Will you help me? I am tied down and I have no time to do the work I want to do. Will you work with me to help others? I'll never manage it on my own. We could do up my old house to accommodate crowds of people, people who are desperate and have lost hope, just like you. Why not come and help me? What have you got to lose? Together we could work to help others.'

This is the basis of the whole Emmaus movement. Those who have been injured and scarred by life will not be healed by pity and charity but by recognising that we need them, by having enough confidence in them and respect for them to ask for their help, by working side by side with them and recognising that they have as much to offer to us as we do to them.

Emmaus isn't some government aid scheme, a good deed by the trade unions or the Church. It's something that 'just happened' to an 'accidentally elected public representative' and a 'failed suicide', as Abbé Pierre and George describe themselves. That summer evening in 1949 they were companions — the first Companions of Emmaus.

Rebirth: 'What if we became ragpickers...'
George quickly found somebody to join him, a veteran of the Indo-China war. Using scrap material they built four dormitory chalets in the grounds, each sleeping sixteen people. As word of the enterprise spread among the homeless they began to arrive in greater numbers each week. As soon as the first family had found somewhere permanent to live (in a chapel!) others were queueing up to take their places. Soon they managed to buy some land

cheaply and, using the materials from an old Prisoner of War camp, built several temporary shelters. Needless to say, this involved plenty of hard work for the Companions — at least for those who believed in what seemed like a hopeless task.

Recently I had a letter from Daniel, who as a young lad had been one of the first of these workers. He told me that after a year and a half of this work he had left for good. 'I couldn't put my faith in it, I didn't believe it would last', he wrote, adding modestly, 'I probably hadn't been desperate enough to be able to believe in it. It was people like Eugene and the others who founded Emmaus. They put their faith in it and worked for it....'

Women were also involved in the early stages, women like Lucie Coutaz.... In the original community, we needed a worker of exceptional calibre to take charge. Abbé Pierre's former secretary, Lucie, courageously took on this unexpected role.

She was, at the time, around fifty, untiring and capable, with sparkling eyes and a ready tongue in her head. She would think nothing of stopping between writing official documents or letters to ministers to go out and throw a bucket of cold water over the head of a drunk who was becoming troublesome, or to intervene between two fighting men who looked as if they would kill each other.

Being threatened with a kitchen knife was nothing to her, she would brush all drama aside in a wave of common sense. Some of the Companions laughingly christened her 'Lucie the Terrible'! Yet despite this apparent ingratitude, we appreciated her presence: many lost and bewildered souls, approaching despair, were comforted by and found hope in her practical, loving care.

Abbé Pierre met her through the Resistance movement during the war. The pair are still fighting together — an equally unforeseen battle, this time against poverty — and

Lucie will never desert the cause. At seventy-eight years of age, she dismisses her hard work with the claim that 'Emmaus was just something that happened to us'.

What did the founders of Emmaus do for money, you ask? After all, all these people had to be fed and looked after. To begin with, Abbé Pierre's parliamentary salary covered the bills, but only if everyone lived economically.

We got by like this for two years. Then, in the autumn of 1951, disaster struck! Refusing to vote for a change in the electoral system, Abbé Pierre lost his seat. Suddenly we had no money. We had just begun work on new building sites at Champfleuri where we hoped to provide homes for poor families. Naturally, we thought we would have to abandon them. Abbé Pierre sold his car and, little by little, all his belongings. But in December, the middle of winter, there were eighteen Companions and the food was quickly running out.

One evening, coming up to Christmas 1951, Abbé Pierre secretly wrote some leaflets on the state of the homeless and had them printed. He pinned these tracts to his cassock and with an aching heart, the former member of parliament went begging in the streets of 'gay Paris'. He brought home money, of course, but this was not a solution the Companions would accept.

It was the Companions themselves who eventually came up with a solution, one which Abbé Pierre would never have thought of. It was a poor person's solution to the problem of poverty, a decisive move for Emmaus.

*   *   *

Back at the house, the Companions suspected what Abbé Pierre was up to. He was begging in Paris on their behalf! 'What kind of rule is this?' they asked. 'You forbid us to beg, yet you are doing it for us!'

Confronted with this, Abbé Pierre tried to defend himself: 'All right, I did beg, but only to awaken the consciences of the affluent. What else is there to do when we have nothing to eat?'

But there *was* something else we could do. Auguste, a practical fellow from Brittany, came up with an idea. 'I know of a way to make money — quite a lot of money too. But it's not a solution for the squeamish — we could go through the dustbins!'

Abbé Pierre smiled sceptically, 'Now *that's* something they didn't teach me in the seminary — but if you know how, we can try it.'

It was the beginning of a large recycling business. At first we went around the streets of Paris; later we took to the city dumps with our bags over our shoulders, spiked sticks in our hands, to scavenge in the rubbish. It turned out to be a profitable exercise. After a few days we found the bags weren't big enough and we got an old pram, then two, then three, then a handcart.... Eventually we bought an old second-hand van, then another.... It was fortunate that Emmaus was on top of a hill because the only way to start the vans in the morning was with a good push!

We soon organised ourselves to go around from house to house, clearing out attics and cellars and gathering valuable 'merchandise' in the process. This piled up around the house. Auguste knew his trade. Everything was sorted and 'processed'. The wholesalers came running to buy. Emmaus was saved. It was a rebirth.

The Companions became popularly known as the 'Ragpickers of Emmaus', and their most important rule was formed: 'We will never accept that our survival should depend on anything other than our work' — and as a consequence of this: 'This is not a sanctuary where you can run and hide from real life. We stand on our own two feet here.'

The *Universal Manifesto of the Emmaus Movement* states: 'Our basic resource, wherever possible, is our recycling work which gives value to every object and increases the possibility of emergency action to help those most in need.'

Auguste also deserves to be counted among our founding members.

Third birth: The 'rebellion of goodness' or the call to justice rather than absurdity

From 1952 to 1954 the Companions' work flourished. The initial construction of nineteen maisonettes was followed by another project to rehouse fourteen families; later we bought a two-hectare site called 'La Pepinière' at Pontault-Combault.

By the autumn of 1953 there were 180 Companions in three communities and we had, between us, provided makeshift housing for about a hundred families.

'But the more we worked,' declares Lucie Coutaz, 'the more families turned up looking for homes.' Some left their foul slums and took refuge in tents, old cars, anything, just to be in the grounds of the Emmaus house and to be sure of a place in the queue for a new home. But winter came, a cold, cruel winter, and the children shivered and froze.

This was an emergency, a case for official intervention. Abbé Pierre asked some parliamentary friends to intervene in the forthcoming budget, which was being debated by the Senate. Of the thousands being set aside for cheap housing, at least one thousand francs should be spared for 'emergency cities', to provide temporary but essential homes for the poor.

During the night of 3 January 1954, the Senate rejected this amendment. 'Just think,' argued one member, 'in three or four years we will be left with buildings covered in placards saying "flats to let" once their occupants have found permanent homes.' It was − 10 degrees that night.

Marc, a three-month-old baby, froze to death in a dilapidated car. Abbé Pierre heard the news of both events at the same time. On 5 January he wrote:

> Dear Minister,
> The child from the Coquelicots city, at Neuilly-Plaisance in Paris, who died of cold during the night of 3/4 January while you debated and rejected the motion of 'emergency cities' will be buried on Thursday, 7 January at 2.00 p.m. Think of him.
> It would be fitting if you were to join us for this funeral. We are not evil people. I assure you that you will be well received. We know that when you postponed dealing with those who come out of factories and sleep beneath the bridges, you did not intend *this* to happen. We know that you did not know or understand what you were doing. If you come among us we will merely say that 'after this he will know, he will change, he will use his intelligence and power to find a way to make this dream real. When they want to, the administrators have many ways of doing the impossible.' People will know that this sorrow has not been in vain. Afterwards, we will take you to Pomponne that you may see its working-class families, including eighty children in all, sleeping in the forest, and you will see the ground that we are working to buy, in order to bring about our dream of an 'emergency city'.

7 January 1954: Instead of opening a new housing development in a well-to-do suburb of the city, the Minister came to this 'funeral of national shame'.

But in the frozen city death continually stalked the homeless....

29 January 1954: Abbé Pierre borrowed a huge tent from a Jewish friend. It was set up in the city as a challenge to

public indifference and sheltered about sixty people who normally slept on the streets or in the metro stations. But for one poor woman, found frozen to death on the street, it was too late. She had died of cold, clutching the eviction order which had thrown her out of her garret flat for arrears of rent.

31 January 1954: Abbé Pierre is invited to preach at Courbevoie, a town in the suburbs of Paris. He speaks of this woman who has died, both in the Church and at the mayor's office. He speaks firmly and with conviction: 'It is now too late for emergency cities, we must set up emergency feeding camps.'

Two 'Friendly Feeding Centres' are opened up right away. The workers comb the streets of Paris for the needy and return shocked and astounded. Of the 120 people they have 'rounded up', over three quarters are not beggars and vagabonds — they are workers who have been made redundant, families looking for a room to live in. Companions and camp workers alike beg for help. 'We'll never manage this alone. We must alert the public immediately. We must get on the radio about it....'

Once again it was not Abbé Pierre's idea. He took it up and joined in with the work. At 12.45 he phoned the editor of the One O'Clock News and asked for five minutes on the programme. The editor was quite prepared to play his part in the work. He asked Abbé Pierre to dictate a text over the phone and he broadcast it without consulting his superiors. This cry from the heart provoked an earthquake in the public consciousness, not only in Paris, but also throughout the whole of France.

The Resurrection of Goodness

Friends, come to our help. Every night over two hundred people huddle up in our frozen streets with no roof over their heads, no food, more than a few of them practically naked....

Faced with this horror, 'emergency cities' are no longer enough. The first two feeding camps are already full to overflowing. We must open more camps throughout the country.

This very evening, in every town in France, in every area of Paris, a house must be opened providing mattresses or straw to sleep on, blankets and soup to warm those who are dying of cold. A light should hang over the door with a notice stating 'Friendly Feeding Centre: whoever you are, if you need help come here to eat, rest, find hope. There is a welcome here for you.'

I beg each one of you, let us have enough love in us to do this immediately. May such misery give us back something beautiful, the soul of France!

Thank you.

(In Paris, bring your donations to the Rochester Hotel, 92 rue La Boétie.)

By 11 p.m. rue La Boétie is impassable. Thousands of people crowd the street with parcels, clothes and blankets. It is minus 15 degrees!

Around a thousand Parisians, spurred on by Abbé Pierre's speech, take to the streets of the capital. Forty feeding camps are opened, catering for two thousand homeless people. Two churches, a few Metro stations and some public buildings are quickly transformed into dormitories.

It is impossible to describe the reaction that snowballed into an avalanche of action. Students worked as telephone operators by day and by night and free telephone lines were available for the homeless. Radio Luxembourg launched a campaign to collect ten franc notes....

In her memoirs, Lucie Coutaz kept a record of all that went on — the beautiful little incidents and the historical account side by side. We will add only the end result.

4 February 1954: The same government that refused on 3 January now acknowledges the urgency of the 'emergency cities'. The cabinet immediately adopts a plan for twelve thousand houses.

15 March 1954: Donations exceed one billion francs.

March-April 1954: Abbé Pierre receives invitations to travel abroad. He visits many cities including London, Brussels, Fribourg, Geneva, Lausanne and Liège.

30 April 1954: The first forty-eight emergency homes are officially opened.

This fever of action was not the foundation of Emmaus, but it brought the Companions to the forefront in the public eye and facilitated their expansion outside France. It was for them a 'third birth' in that it publicised and developed one of the paradoxes of their work in an irreversible manner. The work of the Companions is no more a solution to the problem than the 'emergency cities' are. They are no more than a voice in the wilderness to goad the public conscience into action, to change society and the lives of all its members.

Good will, even collective good will, can never be more than a detonator; it anticipates the law, pushing aside outdated legislation and demanding new and more just rulings. As a plaque at the entrance to one Parisian feeding camp put it: 'This emergency village is in honour of those who, by their work and their donations, have brought it into being, and it is to the shame of a society that is incapable of housing its workers with dignity.'

This accusing plaque irritated many people. Time and time again it was torn down, only to be stubbornly replaced each time.

Goodness doesn't wait for legal sanctions before alleviating misery. It seeks to destroy the causes of this misery against which it is struggling, a destruction which the law will one day ratify.

The *Rule of Life for the Companions of Emmaus* states:

> Faced with all human suffering, according to your capabilities seek not only to alleviate it without delay but also to root out and destroy its causes.
>
> Seek not only to destroy its causes but also to alleviate it without delay.
>
> Nobody is truly good or just or true unless he dedicates himself, to the best of his capabilities, with his whole heart and his whole being to both of these tasks. They cannot be separated without destroying each other.

The Emmaus movement is profoundly revolutionary. The European Community, which is forming before my very eyes, is making a grave mistake when it classifies Emmaus as a charity, a group of 'do-gooders' who help the poor. The same poor can only be made poorer while a minority is made richer by the European Community, since its foundations are power and money. As the Emmaus movement strives to alleviate poverty, it must also attack the great system which causes this poverty. The European Community must build itself on justice, beginning with those in most need and without encouraging laziness.

4

Friendship that is stronger than death

If you wish to understand the Emmaus movement, you must realise that the euphoria of 1954 did not continue unabated. The movement has had many ups and downs since then; it relives these three births over and over again, courageously, relentlessly, often painfully — especially the first. Abbé Pierre has often declared:

> It is a mistake to believe that Emmaus was a result of the terrible winter of 1954. This was not the origin of the movement. The truth is that, without the work that was silently underway during the previous four years, nothing like this could have happened during that ice-cold winter, and nor could the change that followed have had strength or staying power. Unexpected and unplanned emotion grasped the imagination of crowds of people and brought about act after act of good will during that winter, but in fact it founded absolutely nothing.

The movement that came out of its shell and appeared to spring from nowhere had already grown and been nurtured in the lives of the Companions and had been conceived since the meeting of George and Abbé Pierre, as the latter has emphasised time and time again in speeches, on radio and on television: 'The whole Emmaus movement was born in

1949 with the meeting between George's despair and my fruitless search for happiness without others.'

Does this apply to the *whole* of Emmaus? This victory of friendship over death must be continuously re-enacted. It is the basis of each community and its influence pervades all.

Faced with the suicidal George, Abbé Pierre could have passed him by discreetly and chosen somebody more 'suitable', somebody who was capable and a 'good worker', to found the Emmaus movement. He didn't do this. He recognised his own weakness: 'I saw how vain any attempt I might make to dissuade George from attempting suicide again would be.' He acknowledged his liberty as a poor man and allied it with the greater liberty of the destitute. As he wanted to help the poor, the obvious thing was to let the end be in harmony with the means. It stands to reason that only the poor can truly help each other.

This choice must be made over and over again. There are still thousands of 'Georges' who must be helped and whose help we need. It is all too easy to write them off as 'cases' for psychiatric hospitals or rehabilitation centres. The continual rejuvenation of the Emmaus communities depends on the Companions continually opting to give and accept help from these 'Georges'. No matter what work Emmaus does, in any corner of the world, all the communities are united and revitalised by this belief: 'You will save nobody by simply giving, but only by joining with the one who was lost in order, together, to save others.'

'All right, all right, no need to go on about it', people say. 'We get the message. It's easy.' Don't be fooled! It's a very difficult thing to do. It is something you *have* to be sincere about. Anybody can see through a false friend who puts on an act. And besides that it is something that has to be repeated continuously. With each person, you have to start all over again.

This applied even to George, our famous founder. Up

until his death in 1964, he always declared: 'Emmaus gave a meaning to my life. I lived to love and help others.' But Emmaus didn't give him back his home or his family. Occasionally despair overtook him and he spoke of death; this new meaning to his life was no magic cure. He had to be reassured and needed help. The original agreement had to be repeated over and over again. Emmaus is no 'miracle cure' or formula to cure all ills.

What of the alcoholics? There are no magic words that can be uttered to cure them. Drunkenness is their suicide, a kind of provisional death, and they must be pulled from its jaws time after time.

We offer no magic spell. What *is* true is that only sincere, strong friendship will win victory. Thanks be to God, it has won us many that are encouraging.

How can you be sure that it is always true friendship that is offered at Emmaus? This is the one thing which, the Companions claim, sets them apart from all other organisations, no matter how well intentioned. The following accounts will illustrate the truth of our claim more effectively than any long speeches.

*   *   *

Micheline, a young girl from Brittany, had huddled up for the night over the opening of an air-conditioning vent coming from the metro. It was a freezing night in January 1979 and she wrapped herself up in a few torn old bags until she was no bigger than a little pile of rubbish left behind by the street sweepers.

A kind-hearted couple noticed her as they passed. They both wore warm coats, yet shivered with cold. They were moved with compassion for the freezing girl. They stopped and, after an awkward conversation, managed to persuade Micheline to come with them.

Let's follow the trio.

They made their way to a hostel and this is how they describe the welcome they got there:

> We were met by a very pleasant lady, but once she had glanced at Micheline and discreetly sniffed the disgusting smell of her dirty clothes, she politely motioned that the house was full. It was impossible to find room for her.
>
> 'Not even for one night?' we asked.
>
> 'No, not even for one night.' The door was already closing in our faces.

Our two good Samaritans didn't give up that easily. Off they trekked across the city until they found a bed for their charge. They went home happy in the knowledge that she need no longer sleep on the streets.

Two days later Micheline was back on the air-conditioning vent. 'Why?' they asked themselves. 'It's a mystery....' Undaunted they tried again. Their hearts were full of generosity and limitless charity. They even invited her to spend the winter with them in their home. But the girl, in a sudden burst of energy, rebelled against them. 'Stop annoying me! I'm not going anywhere!'

You are probably asking yourselves why Micheline was making such a fuss. After all, the emergency centres were, in effect, offering the same thing in 1954 as this couple offered during the winter of 1979. There is, however, an important nuance that makes a difference. Even though they offered only temporary help in the emergency camps, they were always careful to stress one point — 'Here, you are loved'. When offering more permanent accommodation this is even more important.

*   *   *

One evening during that bitterly cold winter, I walked along the quays with a friend. We knew of a spot where we were pretty certain of finding somebody sleeping rough. Sure enough, there was a man on the pavement. We made straight for him and, without further ado, told him what we wanted: 'Hello there, we are workers. If you would like to help us, come on with us — we need your help.' He hesitated for a moment and then answered firmly and with certainty: 'Fair enough, I'm coming.'

So the three of us set off towards Emmaus, each feeling happier and more worthwhile. There is nothing that brings more despair or hurt than to feel unwanted, to be somebody whom nobody needs or counts on any more.

If, after a bite to eat and a good night's sleep, we can add, 'We work hard here, but only to help those who need us. Stay with us if you're prepared to join in', then we have offered a reason for living. This is more than ordinary charity ever proposes to its recipients, even though it wishes neither to discourage nor to despise them.

So the man we met on the bridge stays while Micheline disappears. But wait a minute! It's not all that simple. After some time he also left us. He had decided, he said, to join the Emmaus community at Lyons. At Emmaus, everyone is free to stay or to leave as he pleases. A reason to live is something that can be proposed easily to people but can never be imposed upon them. As it turns out, the fact is that some do stay, and not just for the free food and accommodation.

In the Charenton community, and perhaps elsewhere, the new arrival is taken aside after a week or two and given a letter something like the one that follows. It lays out the basics on which we hope to build. Remove the friendship from it and you are left with nothing more than an empty agreement, but during the previous week we will have welcomed the person and become friendly with him or her. Obviously, you can't give out letters like this to strangers; its entire message depends on friendship.

Dear friend,

Welcome to our Emmaus-Liberty community at Charenton.

Here, you are in one of the smallest communities in a movement which was founded by Abbé Pierre. Our most important rule — in fact, our whole life — is based on friendship and sharing in order to help those who are in need.

This is not a refuge or feeding centre. We live on what we earn — but we do not work simply to survive. We work to be able to give to those who are less well off than ourselves. Thanks to you, and with your help, we will be able to give even more. We save ourselves by seeking only to save others, which is the mystery of sacrifice.

We need your help. We need your heart and mind, but also your strength.

If you stay with us, you must be prepared to work according to your ability, including cleaning the house, especially your room. From time to time you will be asked to take your turn at cleaning the toilets.

Working as part of a team is a skill in itself. At some times of the year we are generally more numerous, while at other times we have to double up in order to finish our work. In any case, no 'sponger' stays with us — please take note! We prefer to say this to people at once rather than after trouble has begun.

We work on Saturday afternoons because there is a jumble sale nearby. Sometimes you will be asked to help. Accept willingly, or even offer your help, so that the same people don't end up always doing the work.

For all our work, each week we take just twenty francs, and thirty-two francs is put aside for each person and can be collected when you leave. You came freely and you can leave just as freely whenever you choose.

There is something important you should know — we don't drink any alcohol. Please excuse the suggestion, but we find it better to make everything clear from the start: if you come home drunk, once everybody agrees, you will be clearly and publicly reprimanded, but all in the name of friendship.

Alcoholism is a disease like any other. Should you want to take a course to cure you, we will do all we can to help.

We are all capable of resolving most problems concerning the Emmaus-Liberty community together. We have chosen to do this by consultation instead of giving each member a rank and forming different grades of power. We believe that the person who has most power is the one who provides most service to others. Anyone who is false, a hypocrite, or who picks fights, has no place at Emmaus. Having said that, everyone makes mistakes, gets annoyed, loses his temper once in a while. We try to make this up later by some small act of friendship.

If you should find things you do not like in the community, or feel it is not good enough, do not criticise or order your friends around. Instead, work harder, be happy and seek to help others more. Love achieves more than bad feeling. Your generous lifestyle will soon snowball and your words will hit home.

Before sharing our earnings with those in need, we pay for our food, electricity, heating, the upkeep of our vehicles, insurance, taxes and any medicines we need.

Don't be afraid to eat well and live comfortably, you have earned your keep.

You have earned your bread here, it is yours, but don't waste it. At Emmaus, we never, for one moment, forget those who are dying of hunger.

Sometimes in the course of our work, we are given tips or donations. The custom is to put them in a common fund, no matter where they come from or what their value is. You will always be kept informed as to how our money is spent. You have played your part in earning it — feel free to ask where it goes. You may have ideas about those who are in most urgent need. If so, we would be pleased to hear your suggestions.

(Here we give the practical details about how we decide where to send donations, etc.)

If you need extra clothes, there is usually no need to buy them, we have plenty for everyone at home. Take what you need — but don't fill a suitcase so you can sell them in your free time. Tricks such as this will be discovered and will create bad feeling towards you.

Your past is your own business, nobody will question you about it. If you feel like talking you will always find a sympathetic ear. Please don't take advantage of this by going overboard with stories of the good old days.

Though we have widely differing religious and political views, we are united in one aim — to give as much as possible, and in giving, to shame the rich into giving not only their left-overs and waste, but also into a just re-distribution of the earth's produce among its citizens. Eventually, we may be able to build a new world for a new type of person. We want love between peoples, but there can be no true love without first having justice.

When you join us your brain is not anaesthetised. We are all equal at Emmaus. If you have an opinion on something, it is important that you express it, without in any way imposing it on anybody else. We need you, we need your good humour, your laugh and smile, we need all that is best in you.

For many people, television is the great entertainer. We hope that it will not cause you to forget the real meaning of our life here. Nobody owns the television and not everybody will want to watch the same programmes. We must make arrangements between ourselves so that everybody's tastes are catered for. Usually this is done politely; we are, after all, a family. Now and again, somebody will want to watch a special programme. In this case, please oblige — between friends it is easy to do a good turn such as this without complaining.

The Emmaus movement must never get old.

As you know, since you have suffered also, it is a colossal task to try to touch the hearts of those who are successful, self-satisfied and egoistic. We need you to help us undertake this revolutionary change, which is a necessary condition for true peace in the world.

If we were to wait until those in power stop exploiting their slaves before coming to the aid of the starving, we would have to wait forever. Those who are hungry must be helped *now*. But it is dishonest merely to help those in need without seeking to root out the causes of their poverty. In so doing we are hypocritically taking part in the cruel games played by those who would destroy all humane feeling.

And Emmaus? Many have no idea what this name means.

Emmaus is a small village not far from Jerusalem, in the Holy Land. During his life on earth, Christ

inspired crowds of people in Jerusalem, capital of his country, and made many true friends there.

But they did not fully understand him. Some thought he would take over the country, become king, and give each of them a castle or a fine manor. Then suddenly he was shamed and killed. He was crucified, humiliated...everything was finished. All the fine dreams were over....

Two days later, two of his friends left Jerusalem for Emmaus. Nobody knows why. They were simply moving on.... They were dejected and crushed, all their dreams had come to nothing. It was evening and their spirits were low as they trudged on towards Emmaus. Then they met somebody. The man walked with them and, in talking to them, brought back their hope and courage.

On arriving at the village, the three went to an inn to eat. Over the meal, the companions, who had overcome their depression, recognised Christ in the breaking of the bread. 'He is alive!'

The utter despair they had just experienced had given birth to the Good News. They were certain of one thing from then on: love is stronger than hatred and stronger than death. The true Road of Life is not a path that leads into nothingness; it leads to the Eternal, who is Love, occasionally passing through a little inn in a village called Emmaus.

In 1949, Abbé Pierre bought a house near Paris, which he called Emmaus after the village where these two men stopped at an inn and recognised the stranger in their midst. He wanted to make a house that would welcome everybody, nothing more....

It was here that he came to know George. (Here we put in George's story.)

On that day, without even knowing it, Abbé Pierre

had just founded the first, and smallest Emmaus community, where love was the only leader and the only authority. They were two Companions, just like the two at the village near Jerusalem, accompanied by the Stranger whom they wanted to save.

All it took was a friendly agreement between a member of Parliament, Abbé Pierre, and George, a suicidal man who had failed in his attempt, who decided that in future they wanted only to serve the most needy.

That is Emmaus — what it is based on and what it means.

You, in your turn, can tell these true stories to whoever wants to hear them. You will tell them in your own way and they will improve in the telling because you will have relived them in your own life. You are not asked to understand the spirit of Emmaus immediately, or to let yourself be possessed by it. First of all, rest yourself; get your strength back. Later you can help us towards a better life. We look forward to it.

There are some who stay and who soon become true witnesses to Emmaus and to its secret.

'I know!', cried out an old Companion of Emmaus who sat beside me, driving an old Renault 4 through the countryside in the middle of the night. 'I know!' and he began to sing. 'I know why I am alive...!'

Another friend of ours who has recently set up his own business was surprised to see how well he was doing. He came to offer a good job and an excellent salary to one of the Companions. Christian came back, overjoyed, to tell us his reply. 'I turned it down!' He had consciously chosen to continue to work with us in the spirit of Emmaus.

Our friendship has one threatening enemy — alcohol. It is easy for somebody to hide in the illusions of alcohol but his Companions will try, with hope, to maintain their friendship towards him.

This is nothing new. Daniel Gigan remembers the early days of Emmaus. He was a seminarian in the spring of 1953 when Abbé Pierre sent him to La Pepinière, a community outside Paris. Since the police had banned many from the original site at Neuilly, somebody had to reorganise them at La Pepinière. He writes: 'Every evening, to keep our spirits up, we used to warm a litre of red wine to drink (alcohol wasn't yet forbidden). I must say that it was very useful because the only boots we had were broken and torn so our feet were continually wet.'

Very useful, but dangerous.... 'Our biggest problem at the time was drunkenness. It was unbelievable. On Sunday evenings I was the only one who wasn't drunk. All the same I never had any trouble. They respected me. One Sunday I went away for the day. When I came back the whole place was turned upside down. One man had most of his face bandaged. I was told, "As you can see, we had a fight. It wouldn't have happened if you had been here."

'We soon realised that something had to be done about this. One evening, one of the Companions got so violent that his friends had to lock him in a cupboard until he calmed down. Everybody knew we couldn't resort to this all the time. The man in question, who was just out of prison, accepted the fact that he had to go to a centre for alcoholics and find a cure. On his return from hospital he was welcomed like a new arrival. The past was forgotten. We felt that, to help our comrade, we all had to begin a new way of life together, so the Companions unanimously decided to forego alcohol in order to support our friend.'

This voluntary abstinence, which showed proof of true friendship, payed off not only in that situation but in many others. Victories over alcoholism became more and more frequent.

The battle is never over and continually needs to be taken up anew. Our world encourages alcoholism. As our aim is to welcome those in most misery, we must offer hope to all alcoholics and give them a chance, or risk no longer being an Emmaus community.

The result is frequently a difficult situation. Some even rate it as the greatest problem Emmaus faces. Often the leaders of communities tear their hair out with frustration. Recently, at a meeting, they exchanged experiences on the subject.

Each of the leaders sincerely wants to cure those affected by alcoholism, yet they don't all use the same methods. Each alcoholic is a special case and must not be confused with any other. Alcoholism is a disease which strikes a person to the core: it is one of the most complicated to treat. But on one point all agree — no cure is possible without the support of friends. We must see the root of this scourge for what it is.

Unfortunately we live in a world that is steeped in alcohol. The overproduction of alcohol is both stupid and scandalous. And this is not for want of warnings from the medical profession: after heart disease and cancer, alcohol is the biggest killer. In France, two people die from alcoholism every hour.

But it is not enough to reduce production and advertising of alcohol. Our world by its very organisation (or disorganisation) also breeds loneliness. Very often, instead of strengthening friendship and family ties it breaks up, scatters and destroys all.

And what of the lonely people? What are they to do? The popular expression is 'they drown their sorrows' — with alcohol of course. And many of them quickly become alcoholics.... Not drunkards, vicious people to be despised and mocked, but our brothers and sisters whose bodies and hearts have been seriously affected by illness.

How do we come to this? We are all free to do as we wish. Alcoholism, like many diseases, creeps up on us through careless habits. We must recognise the danger signs. But it is not always easy.

I once met a man, still quite young, who told me of his alcoholism. 'Loneliness is a horrifying, terrible thing. My wife left me, my two children were taken away from me.... I live alone and sometimes spend up to six or seven days without speaking to anybody, shut up in my studio. It's enough to drive anybody mad. Suddenly I might decide to go out, head for an off-licence, buy a few bottles and go on my way....' But when I question him further the cause is still deeper than this. 'I began to drink seriously during the war in Algeria. Before going into action, I was so scared I used to drink brandy. Ever since, whenever I am afraid I turn to it....' Who shall cast the first stone?

It would be unjust and untrue to say that all who come to Emmaus are stricken by this disease. There are many other forms of unhappiness and causes of misery. However, many of the Companions *have* hit rock bottom in this pit. When they wake in the morning with trembling hands, unable to function without a drink, they lose all courage, they are sick and despairing.

It is unbelievably difficult for alcoholics to stop drinking. Public opinion is watching them, waiting for them to go on a binge once again. To the alcoholic, escape seems impossible.

Just as Abbé Pierre realised the worthlessness of any effort he might make to prevent Georges' suicide, we must begin by admitting our utter powerlessness to turn an alcoholic from his or her ways. We must first risk ourselves by becoming a friend of the person and truly revealing our own weakness.

We risk becoming friends, and in friendship forego alcohol for the sake of our friends. Cured alcoholics must never taste a drink, or they will be drawn irresistibly towards it and it will be as if they were never cured. Even as much as a sugar lump soaked in alcohol is enough to set this off. One drink leads to another and the thirst is reawakened. In most communities, therefore, we drink only water or minerals, as a sign of friendship.

This friendship is the same as that which Abbé Pierre extended to George in 1949, that is, directed towards helping others to cure themselves.

Pierre is a Companion who can witness to this. He speaks from the heart, with the joy of the saved:

> In 1964, I began to drink heavily because of family problems. First of all I drank in pubs, I had enough money. I had drinking buddies.... We just drank to forget — I couldn't call those people friends, just drinking buddies. My drinking got worse and worse until friends that I valued began to detest me. When I realised this, I went elsewhere, but I didn't stop drinking. I could no longer work. I was offered jobs and turned them down, even though I would have liked them. I knew that I was disintegrating. I saw myself falling apart. When I drank, I thought about nothing else but drink from morning to night.
>
> I decided to give up drink, thinking of my brothers who were all happy. I got the idea at 4.40 p.m. one afternoon, just as I was leaving work. I used to work in a factory from 6 a.m. to 4.30 p.m. I asked for my wages and left. As I knew of Emmaus through my brother, I joined a community. I knew I would never manage otherwise.
>
> That was 20 January. I decided 'That's it. I'll never drink again, I'm going to join a community.' There I found a friend who devotedly helped me through a very hard struggle, accomplished in an atmosphere of

friendship at Emmaus. Today I am happy with myself. I hope to help those who drink too much towards a better way of life.

After my cure I regained the friendship of my boss, who had grown to detest me because of my drinking. Barely a year after my cure he said I looked ten years younger.

When I went back to my old haunts I found the friendship and companionship of those who used to hate me. They had confidence in me again because I had once again become the man I used to be.

Now it hurts me to see somebody who has drunk too much. I always think of that person as somebody who is down on his luck and whom I must try to help as much as possible, by encouraging him when he is sober. While a person is drunk, nothing can be done. The following day is the time to speak to him. When I was drunk I used to say terrible things, but it was drink talking. The following morning I would have already forgotten it.

Yesterday I went to donate blood. The doctor said I had a very healthy heart. You can imagine how glad I was to hear it — two years ago nobody could have said such a thing.

My first name is Pierre.

For a cure such as this to have a chance of success one must first believe in it, be prepared to be patient no matter what happens.... The leader must try to encourage a spirit of patience and warm friendship. Warm, but not suave and honeyed — rather virile, as you will see. The Companions are not innocent children, and who knows? A certain roughness could well be part of the trust you put in someone with complete freedom.

The other day, somebody knocked at my door. I knew
he was angry. 'What's wrong?'

Another door within my opponent's mind crashed open
releasing a raging storm of anger. 'Henri, you're too weak....
You're indecisive. Last night he came home at midnight,
drunk and falling around the place. He was shouting and
roaring, didn't know what he was saying half of the time!
He was attacking everybody, I came very close to punching
his stupid face!' ('He' was Michel, one of the Companions.)

I take in my friend's violent gestures and accusing stare.
I fix him with the most calm look I can muster. He is raging,
last night was the final straw....

After a few moments' silence I launch my attack — 'And
what about you? What are you going to do? If we could only
be patient for a little while longer.... Remember Jean,
Bernard, Michel, George?...' Facing one another, we let our
eyes exchange the messages of our minds.

It's agreed. We are going to wait, give friendship another
chance.

Three weeks later, on a Monday morning, there is another
knock on my door. This time it's Michel himself. I don't
believe this.... It's incredible! Has he just said this to me?

'I want to go to hospital and try to give up drink.'

'What?!' I have to make him repeat it.... It's unbelievable.
This is urgent.... For once, my work will wait.

A quick phone call to a hospital that deals with alcoholism.
We're out of luck. The management excuses itself. 'For the
past few months, a psychologist selects those who are to
be admitted. You will be put on a waiting list and after three
interviews, may be selected. You will then be admitted eight
days later.'

What am I going to say to Michel? He can't wait. He
knows as well as I do that the flash of good will and freedom
will have disappeared within a day or two. I try again. 'Yes,
I understand. I'm calling from Emmaus. Already two of our

Companions have been discharged from *your* hospital. They are new people, absolutely unrecognisable!...' With the compliment I managed to get my foot in the door. We have a chance. I go back to Michel.

Now it is he who is surprised by the prospect of sudden departure. 'What? Leave in an hour? I'll never have time to pack my things! It can't be done.'

Gently, I persuade him to go ahead with the plan. It is not yet 10.00 a.m. and we are ready to go. Our bags are packed, the car is started up — and Michel is indecisive once again.

My temper takes over. I couldn't repeat what I shouted at him. I must have called him every name under the sun. Eventually I get into the car and start to drive him myself. In any case he doesn't know the way very well. But about two kilometres before the hospital I stop the car. Bluntly and peremptorily I give him his choice. 'Listen Michel, the hospital is straight up the hill, there's a bar here in front of you. Out you get, and take your cases.'

I drove off without looking back.

That evening I was worried. Michel was a good friend of mine and I did care about him. I rang the hospital to see if he had turned up. 'Yes, this man was admitted today', says the voice on the other end of the phone. I go to visit him right away. He is already entertaining his new companions with the story of the day's events. Everybody is laughing heartily and Michel looks happy to be alive again. A new road opens before him.

Four weeks later he is home again. His sons and nephews are amazed — he is a changed man, unrecognisable.

The change in his personality since his arrival at Emmaus is incredible. He remembers the exact day and time he arrived, and even the first thing I said to him. Do you want to hear it? At Emmaus we are not afraid to use crude words. Michel had barely arrived when I said to him: 'Did you leave the packet outside the door?' Dumbfounded, he answered 'What packet?' I looked him in the eye and retorted 'The packet of shit!' I realise that somebody as polite and well-brought up as he, from a very refined milieu, wouldn't forget that too easily! The two of us still laugh at that today.

It is of prime importance to alcoholics that they be surrounded by friendship before, during and after their cure. They must feel that their friends have confidence in them. Usually, if they are not part of a group, whether it be a family or community, they find it impossible to recover.

But alcoholics must also use every chance they get, grasp at the last straws of hope, which, luckily, are always present in the heart of every sick person. It is they who can and must cure themselves.

Then there was your story, Jean. Do you mind if I tell it? With you, we were also strict and hard. Tomorrow will be the seventh anniversary of the day we arrived at the abandoned chapel which we gradually turned into a recycling workshop. (I hope you don't mind my writing about it.)

Together we founded an Emmaus community which we called 'Emmaus-Liberty' and it certainly was hard work! You nearly drove me out of my mind. (Did I get on your nerves as much as that?) But you admit it — it was drink that drove you crazy. You changed totally under its influence.

I remember my surprise when you went into hospital in the hope of becoming the man you used to be and of winning back the love of your wife and child. Your cure was excellent, your relapse disastrous. A friend saw you and rushed to tell me: 'Jean's down there — he's the colour of death!' The man's voice sounded as if he was already visualising a funeral, but we must never despair. Where there's life, there's hope.

Fifteen minutes later I was face-to-face with you on the street. I didn't mince my words. Do you remember? In five

71

minutes flat I had told you exactly what I thought of you. I can still hear your reply, 'You have my back against the wall.... I'm going back to hospital.' It was about time too, and not yet too late.

And look at you now! You are the leader of a community, inspiring and dynamic, truly cured. You like to remind people — 'I'm cured!' One only has to see Jean-Louis, your son, to know the truth of this. I remember him seven years ago, cowering between his mother and his menacing father. Now he is proud of you, and declares to all and sundry 'It's all over now....' And everything is just beginning.

Bernard's story is also worth telling. He sometimes settles himself comfortably in the evening and recounts it to anybody who is willing to listen:

> I had all I could wish for — a wonderful wife, charming children, an interesting job. I don't know why I ever began to drink, I had no reason to. Then everything fell apart, for two years I slept rough and travelled around aimlessly. One winter I slept in the snow in the ditches too frequently and ended up in hospital. It was there that I heard a nun speaking about Emmaus.

You came here and we spent months together. You still drank a lot, though not as heavily as you had been drinking. I remember one morning when you couldn't stop your hands trembling. That frightened you. The two of us set off for the hospital — followed by the pup who seemed sad to see you leave! Why do you always remember that I bought you a new wallet that day? The moment that true friendship begins is unforgettable.

The first month was almost impossible.... You have often told me of how you went out to a bar and were about to order a glass of wine when at the last minute you heard yourself calling 'One coke, please.'

Friendship that is stronger than death

You have been leader of an Emmaus community for over three years now. You persevered in the effort and can now look back and say 'It was another life, completely different.'

Now it's your turn to know how it feels to carry home somebody whom drink has transformed into a human wreck, to fight against those it has made into wild beasts. *You* now have to affirm that victory is always possible, and yet realistically warn that it is never guaranteed.

And how could we leave the subject of alcoholism without mentioning your story, Christian? Life didn't spoil you. You had it tough — what with trying to find work here and there, your health marred by accidents. You were all alone in the world, in a solitary battle against the lure of alcohol. Emmaus-Liberty welcomed you. It is hard to put up with an alcoholic. We loved you, and because of our love you escaped from alcoholism a new man. Drunk one afternoon, you grabbed my shoulder, you were going to break my face. Suddenly you glimpsed my only defence — the friendship in my eyes. Now, after a successful cure, you never want to taste a drink for the rest of your life. You have a lot to give, and a great thirst to help those less well off than you.

The other day, Bernard winked maliciously at one of the Companions, saying, 'I'd hardly know you now.' Back came the reply like lightening, 'Nor I you.' The pair of them laughed together.

*　　*　　*

In France alone there are a million alcoholics! Various movements have sprung up to enable those who have recovered to save others from this scourge. Modern methods are used — drugs, group psychology, spiritual dynamism. The particular belief varies from one to another but all of them put friendship top of the list.

At Emmaus we haven't isolated the struggle against

alcoholism from our other struggles. It is one aspect, often a leading one, of our struggle against all that lowers humanity, against the forces of death. It is not a charitable struggle, but one motivated by friendship. Every morning we take up a new spirit of faithfulness to the first birth of Emmaus.

5

A house of hope

I seek only a place where I can live,
Where I can plant a red flower and sing.
I seek only a place where I can intertwine posts and
    reeds to build walls
And make a shelter that will be my house.

I seek only to be able to rest
When, after my work is finished,
I return home tired.

I seek only a place where my sons may grow
And strive each day for liberty.

This is a poem by a Peruvian inhabitant of the *City of New Hope*. What a call to the Companions, what a fulfilling confirmation of what will always be one of their vocations — building for the homeless. They were once called the 'ragpicker builders' — and not without reason. If there is one sign common to the three births of Emmaus it is that of the house. From the huge abandoned building to which Abbé Pierre invited Georges in 1949 to the housing projects of Christmas 1952 and the 'emergency cities' of January 1954, Emmaus has always been synonymous with 'house'.
   During the early 1970s Abbé Pierre was at a conference in Perth, Australia, when he was accosted by a happy family. The father of the family asked him 'Don't you

remember us? Seventeen years ago my wife and I were among the first families you welcomed in the 'village of need'. We were able to begin to hope again. We got a grant from the Australian government to cover the fare out here. Today I have my own small business. We are saved! Give our thanks to the Companions of Emmaus. We have just heard from a solicitor in France that we have inherited a small house. We don't need it now. Take it and use it to save others.'

Is this all ancient history? Is Emmaus outmoded? One would have to be pretty blind not to see the slums and shanty towns that are stretching ever further into the countryside around the fine new cities in Africa, Asia and Latin America. In an editorial in the magazine *Emmaus International* in 1978, Abbé Pierre could still write: 'The housing problem is relevant throughout the entire world. It will only be resolved when we alert our consciences to it and realise that it is the first of all our problems.'

It is true that the Companions of Emmaus are better qualified than anybody to understand this. I firmly believe in the spirit of Emmaus. If you have a house do not sleep peacefully in it without thinking of those who have nowhere to lay their heads.

Few animals can do without a home, a special place where they can rest. The fox has his den, the bird his nest, the hare his form — the human builds a house.

Since we left our caves, thousands of us base our lives on this ideal, building ourselves houses where we can live with our families, lovingly altering and improving our homes as the years pass. How many people do you know who remember with love for the rest of their lives the houses in which they were reared?

It is a terrible thing for anybody to lose their house. During the war, I saw adults crying like babies when they saw their houses go up in flames or tumble in piles of stone. It's a catastrophe, everything falls apart, life seems to be pointless.

Housing schemes have not altered this yearning for 'a place of one's own'. The other day on television I saw a worker who had just been made redundant. He had tears of despair in his eyes, no salary now, no hope of having a home of his own in his old age.

Anybody who has not felt the pain of not having a place of his own can never understand this. I have just visited an old friend I hadn't seen for fifteen years. I could feel his unhappiness at not being able to invite me to share his meal as he muttered 'This isn't my own place'.

Abbé Pierre has good reason to understand the importance of having a house of one's own. Within the two years following the war he found himself homeless three times — scouring the small ads, chasing from one agency to another. He wasn't long in coming up with the idea of renovating an abandoned house. And as it was too large for him alone Emmaus seemed to follow naturally.

As for the Companions, many of them, indeed most of them, have spent days, months, even years, without warmth or shelter. They understand perfectly what a house can signify. Many of the Companions are former travellers. According to official figures thousands of people criss-cross France in all directions and all weathers. Today, even as you read, there are people travelling, homeless, around the country. The day before yesterday Gerard, a forty-eight-year-old man, arrived at our door at Charenton, having walked from Abbéville. He had a week's stubble on his chin and his feet were blistered and bleeding. Needless to say, motorists don't often stop for somebody in this condition.

They are travelling the roads.... Each one of them could tell of the slow progress, the detours, stops for rest in tumbledown barns, the hunger, thirst, the miles to be covered, the mirages imagined on the roadside (at last, water! but no, just an illusion....) and the anguish of solitude. 'I am totally alone, without family or friends. Where can I rest when night falls and the wind rises to a storm, when rain pours down in a torrent, when snow covers the ground and birds freeze to death?' On the open, endless road, at these hard, cruel times, the house becomes a dream as glittering as it is inaccessible.

Those who have slept in the hollow of a ditch, in maize fields, among the bracken in woods in the middle of winter, sheltered by a bare wall, understand this. It is useless and unecessary to elaborate. They too have travelled, and are travelling still.

There are towns in France where the authorities have had the consideration to build shelters even for stray dogs, while they have been incapable of organising anything to welcome the people who are homeless. On approaching many of these towns, the homeless are greeted by a huge sign which the authorities have had the audacity to erect on the roadside. The sign is eyecatching, but also strikes the heart — 'Welcome to ...'. To whom is the welcome extended? To dogs?

At the end of the road which led to the village of Emmaus, there was an inn towards which two tired and world-weary men were heading. Thanks to the stranger whom they met on the way, they found, at nightfall, human warmth — something which is as vital as the air we breathe if we are to retain our will to live.

There are only about eighty-five Emmaus communities in France. From the outside, no two are alike — yet they all try to retain the ideal upon which they were founded, in order to welcome travellers. This is how it was expressed in a leaflet during the initial years of Emmaus. 'Our wish is to be able to say to those who suffer: ''Enter, eat, rest, have some clean clothes. Then, if you wish, share our work — and therefore our home.'' '

In the space of a few days I have seen faceless, anonymous

people recover their humanity. A room of one's own, a good bed, plenty of simple food can work wonders. I have often noticed someone's gaze rest on the sign in the dining-room: 'This is your house.' The shoulders rise, the person walks tall, breathes easily, suddenly looking years younger.

Each Emmaus house wishes to be a house of hope. Just a house — not a palace! Even today houses can still be a symbol of injustice. Formerly, the castle looked down on the cottage. Today the buildings of the Third World in Rio, Santiago and Abidjan look down scornfully on the nearby slums and shanty towns. Even the cemeteries seem to try to maintain this ridiculous difference beyond the grave. The wooden crosses of the poor strive in vain to stay clear of brambles and nettles. The elaborate crypts of the rich stand as monuments to foolish pride and insolence.

The homes of Emmaus workers do not insult the poor however. Our houses, where people come to recuperate and put their lives back together often need to be reassembled themselves!

An old fortification from the Franco-Prussian war can be pretty dismal, as you can imagine. Thirty people live in one, and witness to the metamorphosis peace can bring about — the inside has become warm and bright.

A commune wanted to invite us to live among them, but where? There was an old disused water tower on their land. Surely it was unthinkable? But within a few months it was renovated with ingenuity and energy to become a home for the Companions.

Another building, a priory, had been abandoned by the monks who used to live there. Enormous buildings, but ancient and timeworn. We had little or no money, plenty of good will, strong helping hands and a mountain of faith. The community moved in in 1973.

Here at Charenton, we made use of a derelict chapel and succeeded, not without some problems and risks, in making a dwelling with several storeys.

79

Elsewhere, a handful of Companions camped near an old hunting lodge. Winter was drawing to a close as they began work, their hearts full of hope. Their task? To make the lodge, which had been abandoned for over two years, habitable once more. There were no windows, no doors, a hole in the roof.... After a few months it was hard to believe that the building had ever been in this condition.

Why turn down this huge, empty gaping garage? It will do the job perfectly. Little by little, people who were once strangers to one another rebuild both the house and their own souls and bodies.

Sometimes we are not lucky enough to find abandoned buildings near a town and are forced to build from scratch, maybe in the middle of a boggy woodland, or to prop up a few tumbledown huts to live in.

Everything can be put to some use. Everything. In Holland the first community set up in two pigsties and a henhouse. In Holland, it must be admitted, the cowsheds have the reputation of being cleaner then some of our farmhouses!

In Switzerland, the first community set up with only a tent, which was used as a dormitory. No water supply, no electricity. It was the spring of 1955. By autumn a permanent camp was built. At Christmas there were sixteen Companions. Emmaus knows how to build and renovate.

It is true that very few of our houses could be held up as models to the town planners. But you will find something there that is often lacking in the houses of those who have much more than we do — the joy of giving, the joy of helping to build a habitable world for others.

The idea of a habitable world is meant in the most literal sense — we work for a world that will finally have the courage to build homes for the abandoned and where, for a start, poor families are able to keep their own homes.

80

A *house of hope*

What more perfect task could one undertake than that of helping each family have a true home, where the joy of children can sing out and flowers can bloom? Abbé Pierre's appeal continually brings forth new initiatives. Four communities of Emmaus-builders in one area of Paris — just over a hundred Companions — have become the 'Good Samaritans' of unpaid bills. They have stood up to the bailiffs, managers of apartment blocks and estate agents. Homes have been renovated and families saved. What work had to be done, but what joy was reaped! In four years, 300,000 francs was given to 260 families, including over a thousand children, who were saved from eviction and break-up.

In all corners of France, 'SOS families' are being set up by the Companions. In Orléans, in the past two years, many families have been saved by loans totalling 135,000 francs.

A few years ago, an itinerant community was settling down for the night. Their abode? A ruined factory. They had to shelter under old umbrellas at night. It was raining heavily and the factory roofs were derelict, yet their hearts sang with joy. By their work of renovation and recycling they had helped to complete fifteen homes for the handicapped. Other communities have contributed to centres for young workers, post-cure centres for former alcoholics, etc.

And this applies to the Companions all over the world. You may think that super-industrialised Japan, for example, has no need of this kind of help. Don't be fooled. The elderly population is huge. You only have to watch Ozu's film, *Journey to Tokyo*. At Mino, near Osaka, the Companions of Emmaus, helped by communities in Canada and by international work camps in Italy, France and Denmark, have set up the Kitahara Centre, a hospital for the old and the paralysed. They now cater for sixty-nine patients in a scenic location with fittings which, although they are not luxurious, are warm and modern.

The Companions always work with one aim in mind — to provoke the rich and powerful into action. Abbé Pierre declares: 'Untiringly, we must continue our provocation of the rich and the powers that be so that construction of housing for the neglected in our affluent society may increase in line with the urgent need for it.'

This is the insistent and unchanging conviction of the Companions of Emmaus on the subject of housing: We have suffered so much from being homeless that we now have the right to torment you in turn until the situation is rectified. 'For somebody who has a decent home, there must never again be the anguish of thinking that her workmates and comrades know not where to lay their children at night. Everywhere on the soil of France we must build homes for our children. Whoever you are, as you earn the fruits of your labour, remember that if you have a comfortable home you cannot rest with a clear conscience, sure in the knowledge that your children are warm, safe and happy, if you have not put aside part of your wages to help your homeless brother' — Abbé Pierre.

But rather than deal out neat and ready statistics or exhortations, let me tell you of my visit last November to the Emmaus community at Dijon, in central France, although I do not wish to set it up as a model of perfection. If you ever pass that way, stop to visit the fort nearby, dating from the period of the Franco-Prussian war. Christian, the community leader, explained the situation to me as follows: 'The fort itself was unhealthy, it was too damp to live in. We found shelter there for a while but for the sake of our health we were determined to find a safer home as soon as possible. Luckily enough, some ground around the fort was available. A handsome building was built there using recycled materials, collected within a radius of twenty-five miles. It has twenty rooms and is painted in fresh, lively colours.

Nearby, two large pavilions have sprung up like mushrooms after a rain shower. Their purpose is to improve the service provided by the Companions to young families in financial difficulties. Christian and his wife live there with their three children. It is the family who leads this community, an arrangement which works well, though only by making people toe the line, some say!

But who pays for all these buildings? And who feeds the sixty or so people who live there?

'Come and see,' says Christian. We set out on a journey. After seven or eight miles we round the last hill. There it is — a huge rubbish tip, which on this rainy day is surrounded by mud. It can certainly look depressing under the grey November sky. And this is home to a courageous young woman and a few men who have chosen to live on the spot rather than waste time travelling from the Emmaus house every day. The work of recycling is carried out briskly — everything is searched, sorted and grouped, down to the bottles and jars. They sleep in an old lorry and eat in an old shack. They have no house — and it doesn't matter! The fruits of their work will be houses that will be built nearby where families can live happily with their children amid flowers and trees.

Since this first attempt is working out well, another team of volunteers is preparing to camp and work on another dump. In the dank and cheerless shack, the smell of coffee brewing evoked the friendship and hope that enlivened this dreary spot. Sipping the warm liquid, I was reminded of the itinerant Companions sleeping under umbrellas. The work, the hope and the achievement continues, thanks be to God.

Thirty years ago, when the members of the first Emmaus community became too numerous for Abbé Pierre's house, we bought (on credit) a place called 'The Reserve' where some Companions lived in tents at first, then in wooden

83

structures, linked with the mother-house. Only after five years did this community have a house of its own. But to ensure that the destitute multitudes should not be forgotten, the healthier Companions decided to set out as an itinerant community with only temporary housing as their home.

Abbé Pierre, thinking about this, saw no contradiction in it, but rather an ideal complementary arrangement. 'There is an equilibrium between the necessary security of the settled community which risks conforming to the accepted norms and attitudes of an unjust society, and the continual recommencement of the itinerant community which has nothing (but which depends on the settled community so that those in weak health need not worry about the future). It is certain that these complementary ways of life will protect both communities from the decadence that menaces all revolutionary movements which succeed in establishing themselves.'

As if to bring my idealistic thoughts back to earth, just as we were leaving someone called Christian to come and sort out a fight between two of the Ragpickers. In English, the phrase is 'to quarrel like fishwives'. It is not surprising that the French equivalent is *'se battre comme des chiffoniers'* — to fight like ragpickers! Christian's wife told me that the men had suddenly stopped fighting. The clear gaze of a three-year-old child had cooled their anger, caused them to shake hands and sent them back to work.

It is time I answered a question that is probably on the tip of your tongues by now, one that a group of young people put to me a while ago: 'How did you come to be involved in this?' Underlying their words was the unspoken implication: 'Were you an alcoholic, in trouble or what?'

As a priest, religious, Redemptorist, dedicated to an apostolate among the poor, I felt, especially after Vatican II, more and more uneasy in our houses, which the students of May 1968 were christening 'ghettos' and 'fortresses'.

Even working as a missionary, the security of the presbytery annoyed me. Called to preach in the inner suburbs, I was allowed several times to 'settle' there, living in a tent, at my own risk.

When I wanted a more permanent settlement for immigrants living in a shanty town at Champigny, we fixed up a shack on some rough ground near the Portuguese chapel. A rough and ready kitchen, three tiny bedrooms. One of us used to sleep in the corridor, ready to welcome the Stranger, the Outsider. We already had the spirit of Emmaus!

Then the bulldozers arrived — ready to level the area. The team disbanded. I found myself with a group of North-Africans at Villiers. This time my home was a shack. I remember the cold, the damp, the flower of friendship that was fragile and timid as a snowdrop. Where was this road leading to? This unauthorised camp of immigrants from the Maghreb annoyed the authorities. Rather than improve their existing site, it was decided to disperse them and redistribute the people to new sites. And I found refuge in a shed that an old couple offered me. They were happy to have a sort of security guard living in their garden. When they had to close up their house, unable to maintain it due to illness, I was homeless and penniless, ripe for Emmaus.

I was over fifty when I undertook my initiation in an Emmaus community near Orleans with forty other Companions. For months I lived the life of a true Companion, sharing the dormitory and the solitude of these broken people. And I thought, 'I have nothing, I have no more than you do.' Some of them sized me up to find out what work I could do — I hadn't even learned to drive yet!

Once I had got my licence I was put in charge of some goods in transit in an abandoned chapel at Charenton, quite near Abbé Pierre. The place could have been anything, except a home for humans to live, sleep and eat in.

There were times when I thought I was dreaming. It wasn't the fact of living in a church that disoriented me. I had spent twenty-five years of my life going from chapel to chapel, from church to church as a missionary. But this chapel didn't belong to me. The only things I had were courage and spirit. Six or seven of us decided to set up a true community, one that would be financially independent. Together we set to work, aiming to earn our keep and provide for ourselves. We never lost sight of those who were dying of hunger in Africa, at the time of the terrible droughts in Sahel.

It didn't make sense to try to set up a community with so little space. Abbé Pierre himself judged it to be an impossible undertaking. 'You will always gather up more than you sell. With no space around the chapel, where will you put it?' And that was his categorical opinion!

As it turned out, since we wanted to remain friends with all the starving and welcome all those without a house or a home, we stuck it out. Where there's a will there's a way, and miracles were accomplished by our ingenuity and determination. It is unbelievable how many square metres of floor space can be created in a church by dividing it into separate storeys. Many came to see us, to join in our work and share our lifestyle. And many left — more than three hundred, over twelve years!

When there were about a dozen of us, we decided to try to help those who sent us SOS messages from all sides. The more we were united by our friendship, the more our courage was renewed. We felt refreshed and rejuvenated — and even physically *looked* younger! And of course we had a house. 'Here you are at home', the sign in our dining-room reminded us.

Our only problem was that the house wasn't large enough to accommodate all those who hoped to stay.

One Sunday afternoon, three of us decided to visit the

retired Companions in their house at Rouen. The motor of our old 4L throbbed along, a comfortable and familiar sound. We were silent — not the heavy silence of the downhearted but the silence which precedes a birth. Suddenly one of the three cried out, 'Do you know what we must do? We must extend the Charenton community!'

Adding up our resources, we agreed that it was materially impossible. What could we do? The only solution was to found a new community elsewhere. We dreamed, but because our dream was born of authentic love, it came to pass.

How many letters we wrote to friends over the next few days! How many steps we took to find another location where we could set up, while still keeping up our normal work!

We were soon offered a house in the area of Dreux. It was an old hunting lodge, dilapidated, with no door, no windows, and a huge hole in the roof!

We rented it and three Companions set out early one fine morning, 8 March 1976. Initially they camped in the grounds, in freezing conditions. It was not long before nine recruits joined them and they formed a community of twelve.

For weeks and months on end, they worked relentlessly. Before they were even able to pay their own bills, they began their work by coming to the aid of a handicapped person who sought help. A little wood, some wind, a spark of love, and the fire took off. A new house, a new community had been created.

And the adventure goes on....

A year ago, a new community of Emmaus-Liberty got under way in an old garage near Auxerre, thanks to a courageous couple. Jacques and Marie-Thérèse, whose children had grown up and married, were looking for new meaning in their lives as they faced retirement. It would be pleasant to take up bridge, gardening or art — but how can anyone live contentedly in his own house while so many hands reach out for help?

They didn't choose to continue their bourgeois 'happy-ever-after' existence. They chose, for themselves and others, the way of hope.

Is it any wonder I became involved?

6

People of love and understanding

Remember Auguste's idea? To avoid starving to death and to enable us to continue building, we could no longer count on Abbé Pierre's parliamentary salary. We had to do better than begging, as Abbé Pierre had just resigned himself to at Christmas. Auguste suggested scouring rubbish tips and eventually selling what we could scavenge, organising collections of rubbish for recycling — in short, becoming ragpickers.

The interesting thing about Auguste's idea is not the originality of it, decisive as it was for the future of the movement. The true importance of the idea was that it *was* Auguste's! Auguste and his Companions found themselves saying: 'Abbé Pierre, we don't want you begging for us. We can come up with something better than that. What? For once you, the leader and founder, don't know. They didn't teach you that at the seminary. We know! We will "do the bins", "ragpicking"!' This proposition, which was to determine so much of Emmaus' future, came from the bottom — it was produced by the group.

Finest of all, perhaps, was Abbé Pierre's acceptance of Auguste's idea — a shining example of leadership!

There is no shortage of recycling work for us, allowing us to support ourselves, found new communities and share. If recycling was a good solution to our problems at the beginning, and still is, that is not to say that any honest work is not suitable for Emmaus, providing that we keep our priority of sharing with those in greatest need.

Even now, there are towns ready to welcome us. Others wait for new communities to open. What we need, basically, is a site near an important urban centre. That isn't the hardest part. As soon as the house opens, it begins to fill with new Companions. Within a fortnight it is full without the help of advertising or publicity. But this new community needs a leader: no community can set up or survive without somebody who is physically and morally solid at the helm — somebody who judges both with the heart and with the head.

Hence the appeal was launched to persuade generous men and women to become leaders of communities.

> There is no city in the world with a population of over twenty thousand that doesn't need a few communities of Emmaus ragpickers, men and women alike. The movement is continually receiving requests. What is needed to respond to them is not usually land, houses or money, but men and women capable of filling the difficult and fulfilling position of leader.

> *The Ragpickers of Emmaus*, Boris Simon, 1971

In autumn of 1978, Abbé Pierre smiled sadly as he confided in me: 'I'm going to go around the country to presbyteries and religious houses looking for leaders for Emmaus communities.'

Priests are still plentiful in France. Some of them seek new evangelical ways of life. Ever the optimist, the founder of Emmaus hoped to meet the volunteer he had dreamed of: 'Just one, and it would be worth it....' One single volunteer — that would be enough to compensate for journeying all the roads of France!

What does a leader have to do? One of them defines the role: 'There are three sides to my function in the community. I take charge of the economic side of things, the financial direction of the group. I secure community life, and I have a personal role in relation to each individual.'

As you can see, it takes more than good will. A leader must be businesslike, since there is an industry to run, but even more importantly, must be an inspired teacher, continually reawakening hope in the Companions. In an old manifesto of Emmaus-France in 1957, Abbé Pierre asked the leader, above all else, to share his blind belief in the movement.

> The leader, also, is driven by the same spirit of love for those who suffer — whether he joined Emmaus as a leader or acceded to this post after some time spent in the community — his life at present is put generously at their disinterested service. He freely decides to give his time to live permanently in the community, with the Companions, sharing their daily life, doing his job as part of the team.

The leader is motivated not by the egoistical pride of giving orders to the Companions, but by the feeling of living through helping one another — he does not organise 'their' work but lives for the love of working with them.

Visit any Emmaus community. You may have difficulty in distinguishing the leader from the others. 'That can't be true! The leader? That guy unloading the truck?' 'The cook is the leader!' 'You're not telling me that this worker with a face as black as a miner is leader!'

A new arrival observed naively, 'I thought the leader was the best-dressed one of you!' It took him two days to work out who it was. He had truly been made welcome by the community, not by a boss.

For a true leader of an Emmaus community there should

be no question of making a profit from the job. 'I've been with Emmaus for twenty-five years', Jules told me. 'I've been community leader for eighteen of those — I am no richer now than the day I joined.' He showed me his wrist — he wore no watch: 'I had none when I joined,' he explained....

People of this calibre, dedicated to total sharing, are not easily found. So many of the troubles of humanity are caused by this division between master and slave, between the dominators and the dominated. Emmaus would be doing nothing sensational or even commendable if it did not begin at the very heart of the movement and seek with all its power to put an end to this struggle that is as old as the world itself.

Eugene, an old Companion who died in 1978 after many years as an Emmaus leader, used to say:

> At Emmaus, we must guard against the possibility of those who achieve plenty and become stars, to the detriment of the 'small' man who takes all the knocks. There are no 'small men' at Emmaus, or if there are, they are better off than the others.

Most importantly, each Companion, down to the most humble of jobs, must feel that he is leader in his own work. The driver must feel in charge at the wheel of his vehicle, the scrap merchant with his scrap metal, the sales person in the shop, the cook in the kitchen.

On the subject of joint decisions, this is what the Brest community has to say: 'We organise our work together. As for money and help given to needy families, it is we, as a community, who run it. We assess and challenge the decisions of our leaders.'

In the Charenton community, when we get an urgent request from another province for example, each Companion is asked to decide whether or not it is a worthy cause. After a few days to reflect on it, we make our choices and a sum of money is sent off — a sum in direct proportion to the number of those who have voted for it.

If, for example, we are a group of ten and have 30,000 francs to spare, we take our vote. If one of us votes against, deeming other needs more deserving or urgent than the request in question, then we send 27,000 francs. The remaining 3,000 francs is free for other needs. In this way, the donation is from the community as a whole and the opinion of each individual is taken seriously.

Why do these communities, who live such a life of shared responsibility and leadership, not generate their own leaders? This would be the ideal situation, but it's not easy to bring about. 'How difficult it is to find leaders for Emmaus!' writes Jean-Yves Olichon in Brazil. 'This requires first of all that the person should be able to take responsibility for himself and for others — a feat requiring patience and perseverance!

'However this is not impossible. Sometimes all it takes is long months of waiting. It is important to wake up each morning and look afresh at the world. People change, for the worse but also for the better. Stubbornly held prejudices on various things serve only to blind a person, making it impossible to look on the world as does a shoot rising from the earth in springtime.... One has to be totally discreet and cautious in order to avoid trampling on these hopes of others. Without care and attention such high hopes cannot be upheld. But what a reward it would be for the Emmaus movement if there were to rise up first and foremost among the Companions, leaders of the communities of tomorrow.'

This miracle is possible. During the eight years I have been living the Emmaus lifestyle, I have had the joy of seeing several leaders come from among the Companions.

Sometimes there are unexpected detours on the road to leadership! Joel spent two years with us learning once again to love life. Then he found a job as instructor of apprentices at the Prefecture, in liaison with the Salvation Army. Let's hear his version of the story:

> I was working at the Prefecture on behalf of the Salvation Army as instructor of apprentices. I was about to be put on the permanent payroll. My situation was improving — but I felt depressed and apathetic about the future. It was as if I was up against a brick wall! A 'servant of God' (that's one of the ranks in the Salvation Army), told me to 'Pray, keep praying and the Lord will hear your cry.' And what happened? Two days later who should I see arriving but Abbé Pierre himself! I thought I was dreaming. We fell into each other's arms. He had also been worried about me. What had he come for? To ask me to be leader of an Emmaus community! I agreed and the future immediately brightened.

I covered 800 kilometres in an old Citroën Diane to pay a friendly visit to Joel. His smile, his good humour, speak volumes. He has found his niche in life — that of a servant of all so that each may blossom more fully. We stroll around the garden of the small property he has just moved into. Visibly happy and relaxed, other Companions wander about. Suddenly Joel stops and says to me: 'Henri, I told the Companions I was walking with them. *With* them — not above them or even beside them, but *with* them! Henri, now I am really living!'

When one or other of these Companions, with whom I have walked, also decides to walk with others, how marvellous this is for me. I wrote about it in a letter in February 1978 to another Companion and friend who was himself about to take up the leadership of a community. A few joking friends called the letter my 'last will and testament'! Rather, it was a covenant between us.

Jean,

You know of my friendship for you — frank and sincere. It goes back years and is still growing. We met six years ago — on 11 February, as far as I remember. You can even specify the time of our first friendly handshake. At that instant we exchanged looks. Neither of us possessed a single thing. We were sheltering in an abandoned chapel, with no resources other than our courage and our spirit.

Unconsciously at first probably, a common ideal united us — that of building a new Emmaus community. We had both come from a community and were eager for human warmth and friendship, for sharing, for frank comradeship, above all for peace. I believe we were both seriously thinking of those less well off than ourselves.

We had to scrimp and save in order to keep going. Beginning was hard...the first wavering, stumbling steps.... Do you remember the first balls of cloth, paper, cardboard that we tried to sell to save us from begging for food.

How far we have come since then! We have had our ups and downs of course. But our obstinate tenacity, our rough but sincere friendship has overcome all difficulties. Disgust, even despair, has been forced to give way to an unshakeable trust in human nature. We now know, because we have learned, that it is never permissible to say 'Nothing can be done with this person....'

Friendship works miracles, achieves sensational changes. We know, of course, that everything is fragile when conceit and pride invade the human heart. But it is also true that two friends are an impregnable tower, and even more than that — they are an inexhaustible source of energy when their friendship is turned towards helping others. Today, faced with the decision you are about to take, I want to renew this friendship for you, not by using words, but by exchanging looks. In this way I hope to give you the best of myself.

Yes.... Go on.... You can do it.... You can begin a community. But remember that a worthwhile beginning, if it is to mean anything, must be undertaken *with* somebody, with the Companion who suffers most. In your eyes he or she must perceive an unshakeable trust. (The slightest doubt must not flicker in your heart.) He must see in you a confidence which is rooted in love, which honestly wishes for the happiness of the other person, of all others.

I have repeated it to you a thousand times: a community cannot begin in any other way — and the community must begin anew every morning. Remember that. All the rules and the best projects in the world mean nothing without this contagion of love. Either the virus is present or it is not.

But you, I think, you are capable of spreading the virus — of beginning an epidemic of goodness that will flow out around you.

Abbé Pierre inserts the following here: 'Love has one sign which guarantees that you are not lying to yourself. You must be able to say "When you suffer, I am hurt and everything in me moves to help you as if it were to save myself, whether it is moral, physical or spiritual suffering." I would add to his words: never forget that the member of the community who is most lacking will always be you to the extent that you fail to love enough. A boss or leader of men can keep slaves by crushing them underfoot. People who will follow like sheep are numerous. But is a community a fearful group to be led by the nose?

Your friendship, on the other hand, must raise people up, make them responsible and capable. You must increase their responsibility to provoke in them the joy of inventing, of creating friendship — and always beginning with the most despised of the Companions, the 'hopeless case'. Does not every one of us have in his heart a corner that is covered in pebbles, impervious to all deep changes? All it takes to turn everything around is one day to meet a friend.

It is not with a team of twelve or fifteen people, or with twenty-five or fifty, that you must begin. A community begins with the friendship of two unhappy people who want to tear somebody away from the maze of stupidity that is the egoistic life. Then the wish to create a community is born in the heart — the wish for a community on the scale of the entire universe.... 'Will we know how to see the thirst for friendship and the cry and the hope of all humanity in the eyes of the least of our brothers?' (Abbé Pierre in *Faims et Soifs des Hommes*, no. 24)

Without doubt, you will say one day: 'We're full up. The house is too small — it's impossible to take any more.' But I know that you will never tell anyone that, without that person knowing he can count on you and on all your friends being united in the desire to say, 'No, we cannot be happy without you!'

As I have said, there's no plain sailing even after you start. You will be continually starting over, renewing your friendships with those who are in great misery and who cry out in loneliness or disgust at their oppression.

As I say, Jean, it is by sharing responsibility that slowly, little by little, this common soul will form itself, this community of friends who can depend on one another — *no matter what happens* — to do a worthwhile job — achieving more justice and more love.

Pollution does exist! There is nothing more deadly than suspicion to exterminate the seed of life. Equally, there is nothing more comforting and revitalising than 'I need you — I'm depending on you.' This trust is inseparable from the risk of great and small betrayals. You must teach people to walk tall, not to cringe. Open your eyes, let time do its work. Do not pull the unripe corn on the pretext of making it grow more quickly. But believe me, your trust, wisely and prudently given in increasing proportion to everyone, will work miracles of growth.

— A person unable to speak or smile on arrival, crushed by the hardship of days and nights spent on the roads, will eventually open his heart to friendship.

— Another, incapable of taking any initiative in his work, humiliated to the point of insignificance, will also in time show the true qualities of a person of love and understanding.

— Someone else, a subject of ridicule, drowned in alcohol, battered by this disease that is so difficult to cure, will one day reappear, alive and well from her tomb.

What patience you will need, especially for the bad days, when everything goes wrong, when everything gets entangled in a confusion that would make you lose your mind. There are times when it is impossible to be optimistic.

There are days when everything happens together, you feel you can take no more, everything goes wrong — maybe a car accident, buyers who don't pay up, one or more Companions get drunk, a friend lets you down....

These unlucky days are rare, but it only takes one

day to lose confidence in yourself and others.

At these black and stormy times, you can only wait. Try to sleep if you can, until you can take over the helm and take the team in hand once again.

If you lose the key to success you will always find it again in your heart. When you don't know what to do, just try repeating sincerely 'I need you.' The intuition of your heart will tell you who to approach with these words.

The conceited, despotic, begrudging leader will never have any luck. She will never build a true Emmaus community. She will remain only the boss of a group of juxtaposed people without personal relationships.

What a joy and what a reward for you if, one day, you sense that your comrades in the war against poverty, knowing they have earned thousands of pounds, react contrary to the norm and, freely, after consultation, decide to make donations. This may be seen as simply giving back to those whom the rich have robbed.

Yes, you can do it. If you can love and forget selfishness, a good and happy house may develop. Not a house where every man is for himself but one with a community spirit. Not a house open to some, but one that is open to each human being, our brothers and sisters, that each may grow in human kindness. The Earth is for humankind, for all humankind.

Let us be truthful — though the truth may be bitter — friendship is demanding!

In return, let each person speak the truth to you. Never be a distant leader. The only cure for the fear of being taken advantage of is to come down from your pedestal — to face the fear of being equal. Alone, two unhappy people who become partners in alleviating the poverty of others can be the living seed of the *true*

community of tomorrow, which will claim the earth
as its own....'

(Charenton, December 1978)

7

Emmaus: alibi or provocation?

To the Friends of Emmaus...

In particular to the 'committees of Friends' who have
been kind enough to stand security for us under the
terms of the 1901 Act, to assure our existence.

To the groups of Friends of Emmaus who act on their
own account according to the spirit of Abbé Pierre,
especially those who imitate the Companions by taking
up the work of recycling in their spare time.

To the young Friends in international camps who show
no hesitation in coming from time to time to help out
our permanent communities.

Why do I dedicate this chapter in particular to you? Why
'Emmaus: alibi or provocation'? Because you are in the ideal
position to help us tackle the question of ambiguity in our
work. How can this be done? We must live the mystique
of the movement together. You must be with us and we
with you. 'What I live for' depends also on you.
    Not everybody feels sympathetic towards Emmaus. Those
who ask 'What are you doing?' are not always well-disposed
towards us. The question is often asked bitterly or derisively.
'What do you think you're doing? You are anaesthetising
poverty. You are delaying the revolution by deadening the

pain of the destitute. You are perpetuating injustice by making it barely tolerable.'

Alas, the accusation is explicitly voiced, as the following, taken from different sources, show:

> Abbé Pierre's work is firmly ensconced in the (capitalist) system and offers no possibility of breaking with the powers that be. It does not in any way disturb the status quo, and even lightens the burden of work on the state.... Emmaus tends rather to appease the exploited and put down social conflict.... It is an ambiguous enterprise, an enthusiastic undertaking that bodes no danger for the army of profiteers...a movement on the margins of the new currents of thought which deal with the problem of achieving integral freedom for everyone.

Throughout these unkind allegations the question is crudely put to us, but also to you, Friends: 'Is Emmaus to be a conformist group called to fulfil a function designated by the accepted economic and social system — a function that consists of pacifying the anger that might arise from those who have been cast aside by society, and of neutralising those exploited by our system of production and consumption?'

Friends, we must not lay ourselves open to this accusation!

José Balista, the founder of Emmaus in Argentina, echoed a fear expressed by Roland Barthes at the time of the Rebellion of Goodness in 1954, when he said: 'We must not substitute with impunity the signs of charity for the reality of justice.' That is how Emmaus could become an alibi for 'charity', dispensing with the need for justice.

Thus to begin with we must ask what sort of charity we operate. I once had an argument with a friend over the economics of our movement. In the end, he telephoned the bank to check for himself. The figures he was given were clear and obvious. Good-naturedly, he drew his conclusions: 'Emmaus takes from the rich to give to the poor.' 'That's not true!' I protested violently. At least it's not as simple as that.

There are some rich people who give to us, of course, but many of them give only their waste. We have found in general that the rich are the most demanding people to deal with. They want us to dispose of their rubbish for free, to go through waste that has been hypocritically parcelled up in clean new bags, while it is obvious that there is nothing of any conceivable use there.

There are rich people who know how to make fine gestures — large, worthwhile donations — but we know from experience that this is rare! For things that have even the slightest value, the rich have more storage space than the poor.

One amusing (or disgusting, depending on how you look at it) incident occurred, which demonstrates this. We organised a collection in a country town, during which the Mayor became infected with the spirit of good will. He went into his cellar and began to empty it of valuable as well as worthless goods. Everything came out — objects which were really worth collecting. But as he offered us more and more valuable goods, his dear wife (who was part of the plan?) put everything aside bit by bit in the front room, except for a few cheap odds and ends. As the generous husband emptied his cellar, his front room filled up accordingly!

Those who give most, and with most good will, are the workers and ordinary people. We know that they often have to give with reluctance. An old relative dies. The apartment has to be emptied. Can they pay to have it removed? And where would it go — to the rubbish tip? That would be heartbreaking. Everything cannot be kept, even valuable furniture. And so Emmaus is called in. 'We have no room for all this.... We can't find anybody to buy it....' In spite of all, it is given to us — and often with touching discretion. The spirit of Emmaus goes before us.

It is therefore untrue to say that we, the ragpickers of Emmaus, pass the money of the rich over to the poor, as if with a magic wand. The reality is beautiful and can stand on its own: ordinary people who have a little, help the poor through the mediation of us who *are* poor.

We will continue to seek what we can recycle, from both the rich and the poor, as we are called upon. But nobody must ever impose this false label on us: 'Emmaus, a link between the rich and poor'. We are first and foremost 'Emmaus, a service of sharing among the poor'.

We are fully aware, however, that it is not enough for the poor to share amongst themselves. The exploiters, those who maintain unjust structures of production and distribution between people, between social classes and even between nations, would be extremely pleased at this equalisation of the working class. They would even willingly donate money to facilitate it, thereby buying cheaply their peace of mind at their privileged status.

A certain Mr Protain wrote to us from Peru, a frank, straightforward letter: 'You can see why your campaigns of charity, good and commendable, necessary and productive as they may be would only be a kind of sedative or sleeping tablet, enabling us to endure further suffering, if you did not direct your forces towards a radical transformation of the economic system, making it more brotherly and more just, not simply oriented towards achieving greater profits for some. It is in this way that we may arrive at the heart of the problem, at the nub of the causes of deprivation.'

It is here, Friends, that we have great need of you. Firstly, because it is most often you who make us known to people. It is by you and by the witness of your lives that we are judged.

We are not asking you to applaud our good work. True goodness often goes unnoticed. However the Rebellion of Goodness in 1954 seems to have refuted this maxim. What fanfares and acclaim greeted it. 'This is a great moment in the history of France!' cried François Mauriac. And he added: 'No magic wand has ever, in any fairy-tale, created such a marvel.' But life is not a fairy-tale and as for the 'marvel', it very soon faded into memory. Abbé Pierre was exasperated to the point of denouncing 'the unforgivable idolatry of those who pin my photo to the wall, spill a few emotional tears and then go on their way, convinced that they have done a lot.' Friends of Emmaus, we do not ask you to cry with one eye for our troubles, to smile with the other at our friendship, while singing our praises, without doing anything concrete. That would be mere sentimentality.

What we do ask of you is to act. Do not become irritated if we remind you frequently of the first point of your Charter: 'The Friends of Emmaus, faced with human suffering, will seek to the best of their ability not only to alleviate it immediately but also to eliminate its causes.'

Let us be frank. Those of our friends who do not carry out this witness will stifle our voice. Coming between us and public opinion, they provide evidence to support our accusers who can claim: 'It's easy to see whose side they are on. Look who protects them.'

Personally, I can never speak of the Emmaus movement without repeating the words of its founder: 'It is dishonest to alleviate poverty without struggling to root out and destroy its causes.'

The leaflet that Abbé Pierre distributed when he went begging on behalf of the Companions at Christmas 1951 contained the words 'give...,give...,give....' but first one must 'fight...,fight...,fight....' and very distinctly: 'That such sorrow may cease, FIGHT with all your strength against the rich, against the state, against international authorities, by taking part in any one of the world organisations dedicated to this struggle.'

At this stage, an inevitable difficulty arises. 'If Emmaus hopes to change, little by little, the organisation of the world — which it does — it therefore wants to become involved in, and to involve its Friends in, political action. However, we would think that Emmaus, as an international movement, cannot and, according to its *Manifesto*, must not, pledge allegiance to any political party.'

If we were to join a political party under the pretext of furthering our 'political' action we would find ourselves restrained. It is a well-known fact nowadays that even trade unions don't always gain from association with a political party.

This principle, valid for the Emmaus movement as a whole, usually applies also to the individual community. There are two reasons for this. In a conflict, a welcome must be given to those who suffer, from whatever side they may be. At the moment in Lebanon, the Emmaus community receives people of all views — and, surprising as it may seem, they live in peace together. Were the community to be affiliated to a political party, the idea of welcoming all would be out of the question.

Besides, how could Emmaus be true to its mission of reminding *all* governments of their obligations, were it to find itself part of the winning party, linked with the government in power? The prophetic mission of Emmaus — which is a political one — would be silenced.

In fact, our real political strength lies in this very fact. Emmaus is neither a charitable organisation nor a political party: it is a force to awaken consciences, up to and including those in the political arena.

The Rebellion of Goodness in 1954 has also been called 'the rebellion against the absurd', and we saw in it the 'third birth' of Emmaus. What this means is clear — it was a call to the powers that be, a provocation of governments, a prophetic appeal for a change in our laws.

Prophets are voices for the voiceless. They are the mouths of all who rise up fearlessly before all governments to cry untiringly: 'Your power is given to you not to serve the pleasures of the well off but to achieve the salvation of those who suffer unjustly.' We, the Companions, aim to be, in the words of Abbé Pierre 'the flea that has jumped from the ragpicker's rubbish onto the minister's table and stings him, saying "Wake up, do your job. With nothing but your rubbish and waste, we have been able to do all of this to help the suffering. And you, with all that you have at your disposal, what are you achieving?" '

(Take note, Friends of Emmaus. The question is addressed also to you: 'What are *you* doing?' For you also, we are that flea.)

We can help one another to keep this ideal. The development in housing laws, begun in 1954, was not achieved by Emmaus without the help of many friends, who have helped the Companions spread their action well beyond the communities.

Recently some 'friends' became extremely preoccupied with the internal affairs of the community. I said to them: 'You are wondering what your role as Friends of Emmaus consists of? It is first of all to take a stand in politics or in trade unions that will enable you to struggle, together with all people of good will, against the intolerable causes of deprivation.

Why do you not come to speak to us of your actions? You will see how similar are our preoccupations — to loosen the grip of injustice and to have those who suffer taken care of.'

Who knows? The 'little Emmaus workers' (as we are sometimes condescendingly called) with the world view afforded us by our network in the Third World, may propose more open-minded, but equally more up-to-date and realistic views than the purely western outlook of certain trade unions.

Action for justice finds its own ways and means of achieving objectives. Concrete action and attempts to provoke public opinion, jolting comfortable attitudes and setting off initiatives, do not always follow the letter of the law. The law will one day confirm and consecrate these initiatives.

A prime example of this is the community near Dunkirk. Due to their recycling work the Companions were able to buy a ten-hectare site, meaning to donate it to anybody who would agree to build a centre for the severely handicapped there. Public bodies heard the call and the centre is now an indispensable part of their work. It only took somebody to open the eyes of the administrators, who are so frequently short-sighted.

Would you be ready to undertake tasks of this nature? Let's follow this through to its natural conclusion. If you are a Friend of Emmaus, do you know what Abbé Pierre sees as true friendship?: 'The real or apparent self-sufficiency that everyone displays in order to protect himself in relationships with others must be broken and torn apart by friendship. There is no possibility of friendship or of authentic love unless poverty of spirit is shown, according to the gospel description, i.e. total dependence on and need of others. Until you can openly acknowledge this kind of poverty in yourself and cast off your love of independence, you will remain, in the worst sense of the word, insignificant.'

If you are a Friend of Emmaus, it is because you honestly believe that something can be done with 'poor George' and with all of us who are like him. You believe that the only true donation is that of giving 'them' the means and the desire to become donors themselves, according to Auguste's idea — and that the spread of such friendship across the globe could well be the key to everything!

In reality, our aim is not just to change the little laws and conventions of our society: we must change life itself, alter the fabric of our societies, and to do that we must move the hearts of its members.

There again, Friends, your responsibility is pertinent. Do not impose upon us a hierarchy modelled on existing society, with a leader who is boss and foremen under him, concerned above all with efficiency and output. If the committee of Friends allows us to live in a total sharing of responsibilities, a truly warm and friendly co-management (which is actually just as efficient as a hierarchy), then we are aware of being the seed and beginnings of a new world.

Uncertain and groping, we are inaugurating a new way of life together that is more balanced, simple, free and true.

Renald, a bearded, long-haired chap of twenty-five or so, commented recently: 'Some people are surprised that so many young people come to Emmaus and stay there. But we are disgusted at such an unequal society with such unacceptable injustices. We seek another way of life.... If we find comradeship at Emmaus, it brings peace to our hearts. Otherwise we must leave the community and face despair.'

This disgust with society is not always disgust at and envy of the riches of others. Marc is a witness to this: 'Married to the daughter of a shopkeeper who ran a fish shop, I automatically became a shopkeeper. From one end of the year to the other, every conversation I heard was about *fish* or *money*! I was sick of it all. On top of this, I found out that my wife was having an affair with an older man. I could take no more. I abandoned everything — shop, car, money — and soon I was an unhappy down-and-out. During that time I hit rock bottom....

I joined Emmaus, not because I wanted to be a leader but

because I *needed* Emmaus. I needed warmth and friendship. I enjoyed myself there and I decided that was where I wanted to spend the rest of my life.

It would seem, according to the accepted norms, that to be happy, you must eat well, be fashionably dressed, own a car and earn money. This isn't true! The only way to be truly satisfied is to share all you possess. The joy of living is giving. Even in the misery I had allowed myself to fall into, whenever I had a little I always gave away half of it.

Now I am an unsalaried leader in an Emmaus community. Emmaus and the hope of always serving others are my whole life. I have twenty-five friends, many of whom have also known the unhappiness I felt, and our work together is good-humoured and cheerful. (As far as I'm concerned, a life without laughter isn't worth living.) We take pleasure in our work and the atmosphere is joyful. I once needed Emmaus; now others need me in return. Those who come to stay here are given the best possible welcome. Anybody will tell you — we are happy.'

By saying this, by aiming for this, against all the values of society, Emmaus is a provocation — an important one because it is this model which may be proposed to the countries of the Third World, who with their traditional values, will help us to perfect it. Abbé Pierre says 'You are not just the king's jester, there to keep the king awake, amuse him and prevent him taking himself too seriously. Your communities are the seeds of a new way of living and relating to one another.'

Some Friends understand this. Not only do they encourage us but they make this ideal their own, in practice as well as in theory. They show their friendship by coming to share our work.

The most enthusiastic of these friends are the young. Refusing routine and custom, eager to establish new relations between people, thousands of them take up the

Emmaus path every year. Since 1956, volunteers from Scandinavia, Canada, France, Belgium, Switzerland and Japan come to work for Emmaus in Third World countries such as Peru, Bolivia, Rwanda, Bangladesh, Upper Volta and Algeria.

Since 1963 international voluntary work camps are held in France, Denmark, Italy, Finland and Japan during the holidays. The young are enthusiastic: 'Enough! Our waste and over-consumption are despicable. Crowds of children, of old people, of the sick and forgotten everywhere are deprived of basic necessities. We must put an end to it!'

While others go sunbathing for the holidays, they take up the challenge of recycling for a few weeks — a life of hard work, of voluntary poverty, of service to others. Some of them really take to this life, which is the exact opposite of our pleasure-seeking, unfulfilling society. They feel nostalgic on leaving: 'Here, life is real, it's sincere!' — so much so that they return periodically to join us in our task.

These are, above all, true friends. Apart from giving material help in exchange for sharing our life, they share with us their youth and idealism. It is a priceless support to us to know that they will continue our work (since we will obviously die before destroying all injustice). They are evidence that we are opening paths for the future.

8

The future of Emmaus

Recently an old Companion was questioned about his view of Emmaus' future in France. 'I feel that it's getting too settled and comfortable. Now that everything is well organised you get the impression of being in a factory. When you enter a community, you don't feel the same excitment. The Companions are just as good as those of '54 — they just don't have the same faith that we had then. It's not the same thing at all.'

Abbé Pierre expresses a heartfelt wish: 'May the material comforts, earned by hard work in service of those in need, not lead the new Companions towards the gradual disappearance of the spirit of Emmaus, towards the end of the movement.'

Sharing this worry, I wrote a 'scandalous letter' which is reproduced here. Some say that I was wrong — but is the future of Emmaus not in the fresh breeze of its beginnings?

Letter from a Companion to all other Companions

Movements, institutions, organisations, all rich in generosity, are not scarce today. How is it then, that every young, enthusiastic movement, little by little, ends up by falling into decadence?

Founders of orders, institutions or humanitarian movements often have the sorrow of seeing the best of their creation becoming corrupted before they die.

What does it take to prevent what is often such a rapid disintegration?

The Emmaus movement began with incredible generosity. The founder in his soul wanted it to be the ultimate giving, to open one's heart without a thought for oneself. But now, little by little, communities are losing what they once had. It is felt by those inside, it is declared by those outside. We mustn't be overly pessimistic, of course — we mustn't close our eyes to the good that still exists.

In certain areas we have become very reasonable and sensible, after the unthinking generosity of the early years. This imperceptible change has finally become evident. And the founder, when asked, is obliged to acknowledge that it's not the same.

It is natural that we should change, it's the nature of life. But is it not possible, without being a utopian dreamer or a madman, to imagine that the generous nucleus we began with might, instead of losing strength with the passage of time, grow stronger and develop to full maturity? If this is possible, it must be through a wholehearted return to fundamentals. It must be through an energetic and enthusiastic dedication to the basic direction of the movement.

The originality of the Emmaus movement is simple and clear. It is simply being with those who suffer most, sharing their physical and mental pain and bringing them through it, while at the same time never forgetting to go back to those who suffer most.

From the moment you allow anything to separate you from those who suffer you will find that there are barriers between you. The group closes in on itself, it loses heart. The future lies in following the initial inspiration through to its fulfilment.

Emmaus! Emmaus! Come back always to your source

of life. Quench not your thirst at the fountain of security, comfortable retirement and shamefully large salaries, but at the source of true happiness, true humour and true joy.

This happiness is found in abandoning selfishness and in the desire to give freely and fully. Therein lies the future of Emmaus. Companions, you who have as little as I, it is up to us today to make this future prevail against all the scleroses of routine and egoism.

It is up to us! The original call was 'Companions on your feet!' Let us not grow rich, saving for a secure retirement, let us not refuse to share what is truly ours — our small allowance, our savings, that famous 'pension' which can cause so much drunkenness and disappointment. Obviously we all need something to relax. But according to our ability, let us share still more — let's always share even from our small personal sum.

Close to us, in the neighbouring hospital, there is certainly somebody waiting for the gift that will save him from moral and physical suicide. He needs to be loved and offered friendship. Death is unbearable without the presence of a friend. Let us give of our last few pennies, share the pound that is hardest to give because we really need it. We must do this not for the sake of *having* less but for the sake of *being* more, of being more numerous, richer in love, a greater challenge to society, more revolutionary because we act contrary to the norm.

But that is not enough. What will give meaning and power to the community as a whole is the same network of sharing and giving. Therefore, remembering our origins when Emmaus was founded for others (and everyone could see what was being founded), we must take up the cry, 'Companions, on your feet!' Demand that all the fruits of your labours

114

should be boldly distributed and that everyone should see the results of the community's work.

For it will no longer be a question of a few pennies but rather of thousands of pennies. That can sting — it can make you think of what you could have but don't! Your joy will be even greater, your enthusiasm more certain. The future of the Emmaus movement does not depend primarily on Friends who will strengthen its organisation, consolidate its national and international institutions, however useful that may be.... The most important thing in the community is not organisation — strict distribution, a hierarchy of salaries, well-laid out plans, rigorous objectives and well-defined doctrines. You may say that without this, things are too risky, that we are too dependent on luck and chance to survive — but is it not obvious that the future of Emmaus is intrinsically tied up with the risk of sharing, with all its dangers?

Companions, demand a community life! It means more than working like a machine in exchange for your food and shelter. It means being totally and completely an integrated member of a community committed to the philosophy of sharing.

This risk *does* pay off! I am witness to that. *There* lies the future of Emmaus. Communities, on your feet!

Charenton, Easter 1979

In the Emmaus-Liberty community at Charenton, we live as a team — as we have since 1972, year in year out, just twelve or so Companions. We very rarely have meetings. We solve our problems as we go along. This morning, after breakfast, before we began work I questioned the other members about the origin and spirit of the community. They knew I had this book in mind.

I tackled André, a former soldier in Indo-China and Algeria: 'You were at Pontault-Combault thirty years ago. You saw the beginnings of Emmaus. What must be done now to remain faithful to those origins?' He sits down. He has been thinking about this serious question. The others watch him. He shakes his head. 'You must realise...the beginning wasn't always perfect. Ask Abbé Pierre about the 'black cow'. *He* really swindled us.'

'Fair enough, but you did have an aim then?'
'We tried to build shelters for homeless families.'
'Now what must be done?'
'We must move on.'
'What do you mean, move on?'
'We must do what we're doing here — work hard to help the destitute.'

Jean-Louis, a former electrician, thinks we should modernise our work in order to earn more. 'We have just sent 70,000 francs to Sr Emmanuelle, the sixty-eight-year-old worker in Cairo. I feel bad at not being able to send more, considering the deprivation of the area.'

Usually silent, Jacques is of the same opinion: 'Compared to these people, we are rich capitalists.'

The Companions of Emmaus are, in general, pretty quiet types. They have become known as 'the voiceless people'. This morning proved the exception to that rule as the conversation became more animated. Jean was on his feet declaring passionately, 'It's not good enough that some communities should keep thousands in the bank. It's not our fault — we don't care about the money. What we earn should be given as quickly as possible to the needy. It is the poor who are the future of Emmaus.'

Marcel adds to this: 'In some communities they don't even know where the money goes. I met one chap who thought it went to the state!'

'No chance of that happening here', replies Raymond.

'Not only do we know, we even decide where to send the cash and how much to send!' He laughs.

Silence. Everyone is thinking about the issue. I decide to set a trap. 'All the same, we must keep something for a rainy day....'

'As little as possible' — Daniel's warning voice. 'Have we not often sent money here and there around the country to help out a community in trouble? It is unthinkable that they would not help us in their turn. That also, is the future of Emmaus. Not everybody is going to have a disaster at the same time. A friendly agreement between several communities allows each more freedom to move on, as André said earlier.'

'You haven't said anything, Christian?'

Slowly he finishes his coffee. 'Me? I agree with André. We must move ahead, towards the poor, full stop.'

Michel hasn't spoken either. He used to be director of a gardening enterprise. After three years at Emmaus and having overcome his addiction to alcohol, he is preparing to take up his old trade in the South of France — so he hopes, at least. Everyone pays attention as he speaks. He is the only one of us around the table to use a serviette. A distinguished man, a polite salesman, Michel never loses his temper.

'Well Michel, speak up.'

'Some gardeners work so hard on their rose bushes and treat them so much that the roses no longer smell good. The bushes produce roses without a scent. We must not be so preoccupied with ourselves, with Emmaus, with its future. Obviously we need a certain amount of organisation and forward thinking — but let us not forget our goal, to combat deprivation.'

At Easter, we sent 45,454.55 francs towards a development and community centre in a shanty-town in Santiago, Chile (a strange sum — ten out of eleven voted on a sum of 50,000 francs).

Moreover I have just received a letter telling me of a water tower being built in Namoungou in Upper Volta, using a team of workers from Sahel. We were able to send our contribution of 30,000 francs.

Handicapped children in Kaele, North Cameroon, were recently given some equipment which we helped purchase. Sr Yvonne confirmed it for us yesterday, thanking us for our subscription of 3,000 francs. We considered it a modest sum but the children had never been given more.

For a nutrition centre at Bassangoa, we joined with three other communities in contributing 120,000 francs in all. On the production of this capital the Belgian government agreed to finance the rest — but without our help it wouldn't have happened.

Michel, the rose-gardener, observes: 'People who come to the jumble sale here often make hurtful remarks. "With all this money you're gathering, you must live well." I think we should publicise all the projects we finance.'

— 'Through this book, people will be aware of what we do.'

— 'How much has our community alone donated in the last seven years?'

— 'In the last three months, 150,000 francs. Around 700,000 francs over seven years. Other, larger communities give even more.

André, who was at Pontault-Combault, hasn't spoken since the beginning. He loses his patience: 'It's time we did something. On your feet! To work, everybody!'

*　　*　　*

The future of Emmaus is also its geographic expansion which has continued unabated since its origins. From year to year, Emmaus gains new ground. In 1979 the movement was at work in twenty-eight countries — France, Belgium,

Switzerland, Germany, Holland, Denmark, Sweden, Norway, Finland, Italy, Spain, Greece, Algeria, Cameroon, Rwanda, Lebanon, India, Indonesia, Japan, Korea, Canada, the United States, Peru, Chile, Argentina, Uruguay, Brazil and Bolivia.

This international expansion confirms our basic belief that the future depends on not forgetting the initial inspiration. To expand across the world, Emmaus remains faithful to its original premise: a poor person unites with somebody even poorer and they work together to help others.

This is how Emmaus plants its seeds, takes root and spreads across the globe. Its story could fill another book. Let's content ourselves with the story of Emmaus in Japan.

Mr Ozawa had run a business in Manchuria during the war. While he was on a business trip to Japan the war ended. Suddenly he found himself dispossessed of all his goods.

All that was left to him was a small shop, near the Kotoi bridge on the banks of the river Sumida in Tokyo. There, amid thick undergrowth, rose the shell of a factory ravaged by a typhoon in 1949. It was surrounded by ruins, the result of the aerial bombings. Among the debris crowds of poor people had taken shelter in hastily-built shacks.

Seeing so much misery led Ozawa to reject the idea of trying to recover alone. Instead he decided to try to survive by helping and being helped by others. He brought fourteen beggars together under the name the 'Beavers' Association'. They had nothing but their own strength. The only way they could survive without asking for outside help was to become ragpickers. They set to work. They sold old newspapers for thirty yen per kilo and glass for twenty yen. Thus they managed to assure their material existence.

That was December 1949. At that time Ozawa knew nothing of Abbé Pierre — but he was living the same basic concept! He wanted the destitute to escape from destitution by helping one another. He even anticipated Auguste's idea by taking up recycling, a policy only adopted by the Companions in January 1952.

But had Ozawa's friends found meaning in their lives? In this troubled period it was much more difficult for a person to establish psychological stability than to earn a living.

A Franciscan, Fr Zeno, who was travelling the country around that time, trying to help the inhabitants of the shanty-towns, often came across the Beavers. On his travels he met a young girl of twenty, Satoko Kitahara. As he spoke to her she was struck by the simplicity of his words: 'I ask you to pray for these unfortunate poor people.' She wanted to see for herself. Her subsequent attachment to the children of these poverty-stricken families made her decide to live with them in 'Beavers' town'.

In these hovels, where it was hard to imagine that anyone could live, there were drug abusers, professional thieves, all the dregs of humanity. You can imagine the difficulties Satoko Kitahara had to overcome. The children managed to overcome their inferiority complexes and opened their hearts to her. Soon the children started to influence their parents for the better. The 'down-and-outs' village', once a breeding ground for evil, now became a joyful community.

Then the administrators suddenly decided to destroy the shanty towns and offered no alternative accommodation to those who lived there. Chased from their homes, many came to 'Beavers' town' seeking shelter. Kitahara's presence made the administrators hesitate a little — could she cope with the new situation? Sadly, she was exhausted and weak and soon contracted tuberculosis. Her father begged her to enter a sanatorium. It was December 1951.

She had hardly left the community of ragpickers when they got notice to leave within twenty-four hours. During the night in desperation the ragpickers went to the sanatorium where she was staying and by morning Kitahara was among them again. The police gave in. In Tokyo, public opinion was touched by the heroism of this young girl.

Kitahara knew nothing of Abbé Pierre either, but they were both inspired by the same basic principle — to serve those who suffer most and join in their lives. That is what has the power to touch hearts.

Moved by this generosity, Matsui Toro, a famous writer, founded the 'Article 25 Association'. Article 25 in the Japanese constitution declares that 'The state guarantees to each citizen the right to the basic necessities to lead a healthy and full life'. This call to the legislators to guarantee each person his or her rights is another parallel with the French movement. Lengthy negotiations between the mayor's office and the Beavers began. They were to last until February 1958.

At the same time, hundreds of miles away in Osaka, Fr Robert Vallade, a Frenchman, was also wondering how to ease this heart-rending misery.

'On my arrival in Japan in 1950', he wrote, 'I was struck by the destitution of the homeless and the unemployed. What could I do for them? I was obsessed with this question for several years. Despite all their efforts, the administrative services with their long-term plans and special schemes, are powerless to help a homeless family on a cold and rainy night or a child dying of cold.... I felt the pressing need to act as soon as possible, to welcome some of the homeless, to provide for their needs and to try to give meaning to their lives.'

This is a recurring and urgent theme. We need new laws, but that can take time and we need help immediately. How can this be achieved?

'I spent a while in a Trappist monastery near Kobe praying, meditating and reflecting on what I ought to do. I eventually decided to move into a slum. I didn't have a very clear idea of what I was going to do. I moved into the Shinkawa area, sadly a notorious area. It was situated by the port and all the outcasts of the town and the dregs of society led a miserable existence there. Camped in a tiny room, I joined in the life of seventeen families in a veritable hovel. With them I endured the stifling heat under a roof made of tar-lined paper and put up with the company of rats and the freezing cold in the rickety wooden cabins. I experienced the lack of privacy, the bugs, the mosquitos, the vile odours, the long sleepless nights filled with hundreds of noises — the roar of the steelworks, the continual hooting of the trains, dogs barking, children crying, husbands and wives fighting, quarrels and brawls over money, girls, drugs.... One day I found a fellow inhabitant frozen to death, crouched in the box where he had been sleeping. The following day, I met a man on the point of desperation who had just been let out of prison and who was attempting to throw himself under a train.

In the beginning I felt very isolated and lonely. The first reaction of those in the slums was one of suspicion and distrust towards any outsider who came to live among them. Little by little, however, the children were won over and the adults came to regard me as a friend. All the problems of the people filed in and out of my little room: somebody looking for a home, someone else looking for work.... But I still didn't know what form my action might take.'

This was the same doctrine as that of Kitahara, all that was lacking was 'Auguste's idea' — or Ozawa's idea. This situation rectified itself thanks to Abbé Pierre's fame following the Rebellion of Goodness in February 1954.

'It was while this was going on,' says Robert Vallade, 'that I heard of the astonishing experience of the Companions of Emmaus in France. I wrote to Abbé Pierre to seek his help and advice.' 'We are going to help you', he replied, 'but you must take care not to become "soup kitchens".

Work so that all people, even the weakest, may have the pride of having earned their own keep.'

In 1954, Robert Vallade came to do a course in France. But what better way to learn the trade of ragpicker 'Japanese style' than to spend a while at 'Beavers' town', which was now well-known thanks to the efforts of Kitahara and Matsui Toro?

In 1955, Robert Vallade became one of the Beavers. He was shown no special favours. Like all new arrivals at the village he had to prove himself and earn the right to live among them by his work. For weeks he pushed his little cart through the streets, gathering rubbish.

'In the beginning,' he says, 'I was practically useless. I gathered barely thirty yen's worth in a day. Little by little I improved, until eventually I was gathering as much as two to three hundred yen's worth a day.

It is easy to imagine the effort required to complete this task. A foreigner in this country, gathering garbage in the streets, mocked by children and enduring the indifferent or despising glances of many adults.

Once his probation was completed, Robert Vallade returned to Kobe. Ozawa and Matsui, the leaders of the Beavers in Tokyo, advised him not to undertake this venture alone but to take two veterans of the Beavers with him. Helped by these two Companions, and later by volunteers, supported by a donation of 150,000 francs from the Companions in France, Robert Vallade began to build a community among the slums of Kobe. His site was a little plot of land beside the Kobe-Osaka road. Soon he had about forty ragpickers working with him. After two years of backbreaking work, their effort was rewarded by the completion of a building with ten upstairs rooms, and a hangar on the ground floor to house the recycling industry.

On 8 December 1956, the house was opened and named *Gyokokai*. *Kai* means association and *Gyoko* means morning light. For the poor of Japan, the name was not poetic: it signifies the moment when one who has forgotten all misery and pain in the oblivion of sleep reawakens to experience it once again. It is the time when the pain begins all over again.

But in this new community, team work, care for those who suffer and the common desire to save others turned the morning light back into one of hope and creation. *Gyokokai* is a word which expresses what Abbé Pierre calls the 'enthusiastic disillusion of Emmaus'. It is not disillusion in the sense of 'despair' but in the sense of 'leaving behind all that is illusory'. There is enthusiasm, not in the sense of 'exaltation' but in the sense of 'meeting what is Real, the Eternal who is love'. In Japan, as in so many other countries, Emmaus has become the place for those who enthusiastically go beyond that which is merely illusion.

*   *   *

We could end our story at this point. It shows enough of the beginnings and renewals of Emmaus, and of how we must depend on the constant qualities held deep in the human heart — love of the most destitute and the sense of human dignity earned through work.

The following paragraphs confirm that this is the true secret of Emmaus.

In 1956, while *Gyokokai* was being set up at Kobe, the 'Beavers' town' was still under threat in Tokyo. Kitahara's health was deteriorating from month to month. Eventually, the mayor's office yielded. A document was signed on 23 January 1958. The Beavers were granted 16,000m^2 of land on an embankment, with a long-term loan to finance it. The community was saved. Kitahara, however, was dying. She raised herself to see the deeds, but never saw the new foundation. She died within a few days.

Her funeral was a tribute to her work. A huge crowd gathered, people of all social classes, of all religious beliefs, come to pay tribute to the Christian who gave her life for the poor. Matsui Toro wrote an account of her life, in which he called her the 'Madonna of the Tokyo ragpickers'.

Today, 'Beavers' town' has been freed from the fear and insecurity of those early days beside the Sumida river. Around the little chapel which Kitahara requested, dormitories, dining-rooms, family houses, modern bathrooms and eight hundred square metres of work sites have developed in the past ten years.

The advice and help of numerous people have facilitated a better standard of living, but it was the ragpickers themselves who worked and encouraged one another in order to put an end to such misery.

Supported by the memory of Kitahara, of whom they all still speak, they don't want to consider the Beavers as merely a self-sufficient, friendly recycling association. They don't want to work for their own happiness and well-being alone. For those who suffer more than they, for those who are even poorer than themselves, they have established a service offering help and financial aid, and a free hostel. For those who want to find work outside again, they offer career advice. At the request of the locals, they have set up a crèche for babies.

In 1969, the first worldwide meeting of Emmaus was held in Berne, Switzerland. At that time, the 'Beavers' town' community applied to become part of the International Emmaus Movement. It undertook to bring a worldwide dimension to its work of social service by uniting with all the Emmaus communities in the world. From then on it was renamed the 'New Beavers' town'.

If there are those who still question the future of Emmaus, after such a story, let them read again the words of Abbé Pierre:

If, by a stroke of some magic wand, all of Emmaus was to disappear in the morning, all that would be needed would be for somebody relatively privileged, ashamed of his good fortune compared to the misery of others, to come across a person who feels worthless and despairing, and that both of them should see a parent crying at the lack of food and shelter for its child. Sharing a common thought, the privileged and the despairing person need only say to one another, 'What can we do together, immediately, to dry these tears?' and all of Emmaus would have been reborn.

EPILOGUE

Seventeen years later

In 1989 the Emmaus movement celebrated forty years of existence. It was in August 1949 that the first community was founded at Neuilly-Plaisance, in the suburbs of Paris. Abbé Pierre and George met and decided to serve those less fortunate than they. There is a Chinese proverb, 'All the flowers of tomorrow are held in the seeds of today.' This first community was the seed of all the communities which have now spread throughout thirty countries, communities for which there is still, unfortunately, a great need.

In 1983, incapacitated by a stroke, I had to give up my place as leader of a community to somebody younger than I. I was sixty-three years of age. A few months later, when my health improved, I went to Portugal where I lived for two years, visiting 250 different locations, giving over a thousand speeches. With the help of the Portuguese edition of this book, I spread the message of Emmaus. As a foreigner in that country I knew I was incapable of founding an Emmaus community. Soon after my visit began, a group of friends gathered together, determined to found an Emmaus-Liberty community in their country.

The work was long and arduous. How many meetings were held over four long years! Just before I left for Brazil in 1984, I was invited to appear on television in Portugal. The journalist's final question took me by surprise: 'What have you brought with you from France to found an

127

Emmaus community here in Portugal?' I answered truthfully: 'Two pairs of shoes, two pairs of socks, two pairs of trousers, two shirts, a coat and a hat — nothing more. I believe the Emmaus movement will come from the hearts of the Portuguese.' Among the thousands of viewers around the country, one woman was paying particular attention. The owner and headmistress of a college, she decided that very night to leave it all, to sell everything in order to set up the first Emmaus-Liberty community in her country.

As promised, I went to Portugal in November 1988, to live and work for a month among the first Portuguese Companions of Emmaus. The experience was enjoyable. the Companions of Emmaus-Liberty at Charenton in France, learning of the community at Canegas, in the suburbs of Lisbon, decided to buy their friends a New Year's present to mark the beginning of 1989. They spent 10,000 francs on a dairy cow called Marguerite. Is this not the way in which a true European Community could be created — through sharing, even among the most destitute? I have just spent the month of May living near Porto. There also, an Emmaus community is being set up.

In Brazil, where I lived for a year and a half during 1984/85, I also spoke of the Emmaus movement. There also, the seed germinated. The latest news from Joa Benevidisde Rosario, the founder, is bursting with hope. The Emmaus-Equality community, as it is known by the Brazilians, has extraordinary dynamism. Already the original Emmaus-Equality community has founded three other communities.

Two young people, one Polish, one German, are at present translating this book into their native languages. Everywhere that there is a need for the Emmaus movement, it must take root and grow.

At sixty-nine years of age, I am learning English with difficulty and patience in the hope of one day being able to pass on the message of Emmaus in Ireland, where I have been welcomed with great hospitality and friendship three times already. In Ireland, I will never found a community: I hope that the Irish themselves may found one.

During my last stay in Belfast, I was out walking at 9.00 a.m. when I met two poor people, just like the thousands of others throughout the world. This pair was seated uncomfortably on the kerb of a small garden. I saw their need and went quickly to a nearby bakery to buy a cake with raisins. Returning to them, I shared it…. One of them wrote on the first page of my Bible: 'Everything that is happening here is meaningless. It is all simply for power and money.' The poor have ideas that are more valuable than gold. All it takes for the Emmaus movement to begin is somebody who is not content to be happy while others suffer. Assistance and paternalism are not part of the picture. It is something more profound than this, as Abbé Pierre has often repeated: 'It is dishonest to help ease poverty and misery without simultaneously combatting its causes.' We need peace and love, but based solidly on justice. In the achievement of this vital and urgent change, the poor themselves have an essential role to play. We must be *with* them.

During my travels in Portugal, Brazil and Ireland, the community at Charenton has survived. Following my forced retirement Artenzio Galli, a courageous Companion with extraordinary calm and humanity, took over the leadership. The community had six good years of hospitality, work and sharing. At retirement age, a heart condition obliged him also to resign. The Emmaus-Liberty community at Charenton was in danger of being closed down for want of a leader. At the eleventh hour, a young law graduate surprised us all by deciding to become a leader at Emmaus rather than a lawyer.

Now, twenty-four months later, he states his position in a letter to his many friends. It seems to make an ideal conclusion for *Rags to Riches*. Perhaps on reading it, you, like Maria da Fe in Portugal or Joa Benevides in Brazil, will decide to found an Emmaus community in Ireland.

20 June 1989

Dear friends,

It has been quite a while since I last shared with you news of my life with the Companions here at the Emmaus-Liberty community in Charenton. It is already over a year since I wrote to you telling of my arrival here. Today, despite the twin burdens of responsibility and of routine, I am still as enthusiastic as ever in sharing my life with those in most need. I hope I bring them something, and I know they have given me a lot.

Emmaus is a wonderful venture begun by Abbé Pierre forty years ago. The most important thing he did, in my opinion, was to spread the desire to share among the poorest of the poor, who can teach a thing or two about this to many well-off people. I must say that very few of the well-off people I know would undertake the work done by most of my Companions, especially if they had been through what most of these have suffered. The work is often hard, tiring, repetitious, dirty and tedious, but has a thrilling side to it. My greatest joy is to see my Companions taking an interest in, and even becoming impassioned about, what they are doing for the ideal of 'serving first those who suffer most'.

We draw no salaries here. I live like the others, free of hierarchical privileges. I aim to entrust each Companion with the greatest possible range of responsibilities and initiatives. Many succeed admirably, even at the cost of great patience and growth in humanity.

The sale of our goods is now totally in the hands of the Companions, whom I encourage and help to remain honest and scrupulous in their dealings. This isn't easy when one earns so little, but it is a challenge which has meaning only in the context of the ideal of sharing.

It is forty years since Abbé Pierre founded Emmaus, giving his life totally to it. How strong we would be today if we could do likewise! Unfortunately, the search for material goods and security often stifles our deep thirst for the radical enterprise of human solidarity with the poorest of the poor.

Nineteen years ago this Emmaus-Liberty community was born, under the leadership of Henri Le Boursicaud. In search of a coherent and demanding life we chose the following:

— a simple life, without material luxuries, in order to help the destitute as much as possible;

— that the leaders should draw no salary, so that they might remain a challenge to us, inciting us to retain our conviction, to convince and inspire others. Who is to say when we have given enough of our resources, culture and skills to those in most need?

— to seek a real and complete solidarity with those in most need, in the Fourth World, Third World, through the international Emmaus movement and through other communities and associations;

— to lead a free life, liberated from all that enslaves our humanity, in particular drugs, alcohol, violence and deceit — of ourselves and others. Many of the Companions and all of the leaders at Emmaus-Liberty voluntarily abstain from all alcohol, both within the community and outside, in solidarity with those who suffer from anguish, loneliness and alcoholism;

— to lead a friendly communal life where paternalism

131

and exploitation have no place. This means that we are surrounded only by true friends who recognise the benefits they are gaining from meeting and working with their Companions. No act of personal interest or charity which determines the direction of the community will be undertaken by an individual simply because it pleases him;

— to lead a communal life, sharing the same standard of living, the same conditions as those who frequently have lost everything and who struggle and work for those who are destitute. We offer a way of life, not only to the Companions whom life has treated harshly, but to the entire world that has forgotten the happiness generated by sharing.

It is a year since I arrived at Emmaus-Liberty. We work here with the spirit of change of a revolution and with the spirit of love of the Gospels. I am a Christian myself, and greatly admire the non-denominational nature of the movement, which respects and tolerates the expression of different beliefs.

Today we can speak freely of politics, profess our religion or atheism, celebrate and pray together and fight racism from the heart of the community by carefully respecting the *International Manifesto of Emmaus*. It gives me great pleasure to share my faith with those who have the desire and the strength in their heart of hearts to express all of that.

Above all else, Emmaus is for me a school where I learn to look at others with the eyes of the heart. When I meet people who have suffered, whose lives have been like a chamber of horrors, it makes me feel small to think of my own sheltered life — loving parents, a good education, the opportunity for third-level studies, the ability to make good friends in a healthy environment....

I remember once, when I was young, being so happy that I said, 'Lord, I am very happy. The good things with which you have showered me are enough. Give me no more. Instead, teach me how to give to others.' And I can now say that I have never been as happy as I am since I allowed my happiness to depend on that of other people. Personal happiness can never equal that of seeing happiness light up the life of a friend. And is it not important to love one's work and life?

I believe that the intellect and spirit of humanity are most important. We are not mere beasts needing food, sleep, work and sex. Everybody must have the ability to reflect on his or her life, on life itself, to discover the desire to love, to build and to achieve. Everybody should be able to build a worthwhile life, rich in humanity and spirit. I help each of the Companions, according to his and my capabilities, to labour at his own harvest, not to remain barren, empty and extinguished, but instead to grow and to offer something of himself to others.

*   *   *

Since my arrival, many Companions have come and gone, but for the moment the team is stable.

On the whole, the Companions now are younger, partly because of my methods of receiving people and partly because of today's pressing concerns. It is sad to think that Emmaus can also provide an answer for many young people whose lives lack meaning and structure, who are out of step with the world of economics and wage-earning and who can find no place elsewhere. It is not as easy to work with these people as it is with their older counterparts, given their total lack of training in general, their immaturity, laziness and passivity. All of these handicaps are extremely difficult to reconcile with community life. Frequently, the community supports and encourages these people so that their problems are overcome, yet they are still incapable of taking their place in the world outside the community.

Attempts to fit in: A Companion left us to take up a professional life, but for the past eight months he has been living and working in a community of young workers. Another Companion who found work near the community failed in his job but admirably began again in another community where he quickly took on responsibility. Another young Companion who had just been released from prison found a friendly environment and has grown and blossomed in a community which lives and works with handicapped people. He has now begun his second year there. A fourth Companion began a professional training course and then returned to the community.

The Companions at the moment are Serge, Philippe, Christophe, Robert, Klaus, Ambroise and Michel. These eight are 'permanent' in that they have been here for over six months, despite the community's problems of overcrowding, of communication, personality and tendency to alcoholism. Jack, a friend who has come to live with us, and I make up a pretty stable nucleus of ten people. Antoine, who arrived recently, has joined Serge in taking care of the washing and chatting up the clients in his sunny fashion. Nestor, a young man of African origin, left us for a job and an apartment which we found for him. Lucas, called 'Clumsy Lulu', came to us from Emmaus at Peupins and livens up the place. Armelle and Christophe, the first couple to arrive, came here from

Epilogue

Emmaus at Fontenay le Conte. They are expecting a baby any day now, and are then going to take up life in the outside world again. Finally Pierre, who calls to mind the proverb, 'A rolling stone gathers no moss,' is a steady and faithful friend who works with us every day. Two other Companions live at Trappes with Ambroise — Raymond, who used to live at Longjumeau, and Frederic, a young man from the area. Dominic 'the lizard' is our latest arrival. That is the Emmaus-Liberty community of Charenton as it stands at the moment — nineteen Companions, twenty when the baby arrives.

Work and projects: At Champigny (12 km away) the shop has been renovated and modernised. Philippe, who is still a Companion, lives there with Claudine.

At Charenton, we are improving the chapel. We no longer gather paper, cardboard, metal and cloth by the kilo, due to high costs. The guest room is frequently used. There are two television rooms, three toilets and two showers now. The jumble sales are progressing wonderfully: our fleet of vehicles has grown accordingly. Our aim is to open another hall for jumble sales at rue du Petit Chateau at Valmy Chapel (a vacant area).

At Ivry, we are buying an eight-roomed house for the Companions to live in. However, all property in Paris is expensive and this outlay obliges us to ask for financial help.

The Canaries: At Trappes we have taken on the work of a Christian community from Berdine, by supporting the 'Canaries Association' in welcoming drug addicts and those recently released from prison. Michel and Jean-Paul have already taken in five young people — Charlie, Christine, Nicolas, Philippe and Jacques. Ambroise works there with two Companions at a bric-

135

à-brac shop, hoping eventually to support five Companions and the 'Canaries'.

LAC project: We hope to build an LAC at Melun or elsewhere (*Lieu d'Accueil Chaleureux* — house with a warm welcome). This is a new association we have set up to welcome all the homeless who are discouraged and despairing. It is an umbrella organisation which unites many concerned associations, municipalities and individuals. Those who are homeless or in insecure housing in the Paris region find their situation becoming more and more catastrophic. Some squat in cellars, cars, Metro stations, even empty stairwells. Official statistics and reports declare this constantly, as do the pleas for help of those in distress.

The Paris region is overflowing with opportunities for the type of work we do. So far, we have not advertised at all. Yet, in 1989 we gave half of what we earned to the many good causes that came to us seeking aid. Our donations were in the order of 600,000 francs, supporting the following projects:

Friends whom we helped during 1987, 1988 and 1989

'Canaries Association' (taking in young people);
Emmaus communities at Sattileu, Hagueneau, Thouars and Poitiers;
SOS milk bottles;
Sarah Rajaei, an Iranian child in need of medical treatment;
The Gogannes, a community of handicapped people who received a donation of 20,000 francs and a loan of 130,000 francs;
'Fin de Vie Heureuse', an association which cares for the aged;
Schools for underprivileged children at Trappes;

'Mission Africaine de l'Espoir' (African Mission of Hope), a relief agency;
Mme Chauley's families in need (50,000 francs a year);
Emmaus SOS families — loans to families in difficulty totalling 60,000 francs per year;
Karibu, a community which takes in young people in difficulty;
Fr Guetano in Senegal;
Bernard Boulang in Nicaragua — 20,000 francs;
Aid to Children in Need;
Comite Solidarité Logement (Housing Association);
Amis de la Fraternité Indienne, a village community;
Association of Lebanese mothers;
Anniversary present for the Emmaus community at Poitiers, 50,000 francs;
Loan of 30,000 francs to the shop at Thouars;
Sempiero Corsu restaurant, where food is free and only donations are accepted;
Christmas presents for the Saint Maurice children;
Armenian solidarity agency;
Clothes for African children;
Emmaus-Fraternity, 300,000 franc donation towards its establishment at Rochefort;
Sr Dedone at Burkina Faso — 15,000 franc donation;
Emmaus-Liberty in Portugal, purchase of a cow for 15,000 francs;
Establishment of an LAC;
Employment of a full-time worker who accepts the status of Companion for the purpose of work;

These are all those to whom we have given material help — all of them people in need. These are all projects which will help people, who in their turn will help others by their work and by their choice of sharing.

Today, it is the time for investment. We must

improve our houses and living standards and develop our work by upgrading our vehicles and workplaces, and by increased advertising and greater public awareness of our work. We can improve our productivity and thereby increase our level of aid to those who suffer most — an absolute priority for Emmaus-Liberty.

We are now concentrating on community life, which necessitates a certain amount of organisation among the more responsible members of the community, and a certain type of growth and confidence which I try to instill in them, even though it is often difficult to succeed in this.

* * *

At Charenton, I have laid out some rules concerning emotional life which everyone must build upon and accept. It is not easy to achieve the level of co-existence to which we aspire. I don't approve of Companions having friendships outside of the community unless the relationship is steady and genuine, increasing in affection as time goes on.

Unfortunately, the common perception of sexuality among the media and the general public at the moment does not help people in difficulty to find a balance in life, the pursuit of pleasure being so far removed from all tenderness, affection and love. This doesn't make it any easier to form true and deep relationships with others, since feelings of anguish and solitude will remain, and cause great suffering in the long term.

On 12 February, an anniversary celebration of seventeen years of Emmaus-Liberty united many friends whose presence warmed our hearts. These people make up our network of friends in the Paris region. Some friends have come to help us regularly throughout the year, like Rémy and François, two religious novices. Rémy has undertaken to work with us for a year, beginning in September, which is fortunate for us. Pierre comes faithfully every day to help us. He is invaluable.

Jean-Louis, who also goes to Emmaus at Plessis, Sucy and Longjumeau, enjoys coming here because of the books, the plans made and the lively debates on ideas. The two Laures, who are very popular, are not available as often as we would like. Isabelle, Françoise, Kathline, Marie-Claire, Brigitte and others have each come to share our life for a few days, which was of benefit to both sides. Henri and Cathy, who used to be Companions at Fontenay, now have a family. They came to help us during a power cut and in selling our goods. We have numerous guests and passing visitors, because I want the community to remain open to the world around us, welcoming all comers and thereby ruling out the risk of becoming a little ghetto, closed in on ourselves in our little world, confined, retiring, hard to live with.

Our president and secretary are discreet but faithful, always available through thick and thin when we need them. Henri Le Boursicaud, our founder, gives us short but greatly appreciated visits bringing with him a breeze of international liberty and fraternity and a feeling of our family's growth beyond boundaries, in 1989. Our leisure is used for culture, sport, relaxing, visits to the countryside, to other communities. We holiday in Foncine, in the Jura mountains. This year we visited Spain and Portugal, to offer support to our friends in the new communities. We have travelled to Brussels, to communities of Emmaus-Fraternity, etc.

We keep special links with the International Emmaus Movement, and the president, Franco Bettoli, even came to our seventeenth anniversary celebrations. Our choice of solidarity across all borders remains a priority with us.

We remain part of the Emmaus-Liberty family, together with communities at Alençon, Marle (Laon), and Berry-au-Bac (Reims). Marc-Charles keeps us all closely united. We are part of the structure of Emmaus-France, in our own province, although the diversity of the world of Emmaus does cause problems occasionally. Nominated Godparent of Emmaus-Brie, an independent community in the Paris region, we hope for their full entry into the Emmaus movement and await with impatience the appearance of new communities around the capital.

My priorities at the moment are to protect the spirit of Emmaus-Liberty, to continue to speak for those who have no voice, and to propose a different way of living from the heart of the movement.

We propose a society based on sharing, where sensitivity would overtake indifference, and if that may seem laughable to some, I prefer to live in idealism than to die indifferent.

Best wishes,
Jacques

I realise my good fortune in being replaced by a person such as this. Jacques is now leader of the Emmaus-liberty community founded nineteen years ago. May Emmaus find many more leaders of his calibre all over the world. Adventurers like him are indispensable to lead the Emmaus communities which, sadly, the world still needs.